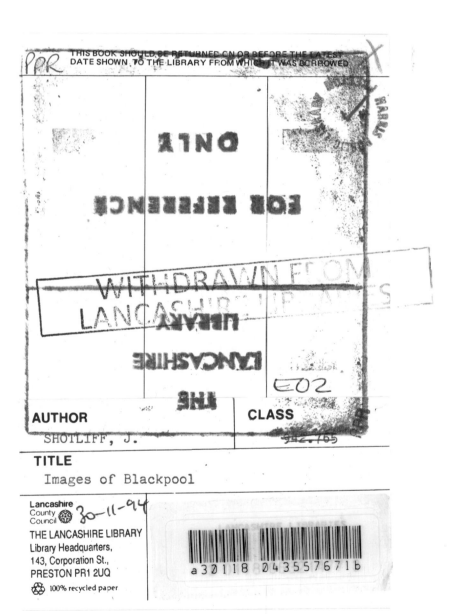

Images of Blackpool

Images of
Blackpool

by Jane Shotliff

Breedon Books
Publishing Company
Derby

1994

First published in Great Britain by
The Breedon Books Publishing Company Limited
44 Friar Gate, Derby, DE1 1DA.
1994

ISBN 1 873626 73 8

Printed and bound by Hillman Printers, Frome, Somerset.
Covers printed by BDC Printing Services Limited of Derby

CONTENTS

Foreword

MANY of Blackpool's attractions over the years have had to be seen to be believed. From the lofty heights of the Tower down to the quaint and curious side-shows on the Golden Mile, there has always been something a little bit special about the place.

And the same holds true today. For Blackpool is a place of superlatives.

People used to flock to see the thinnest or fattest ladies on the Golden Mile – or those with the most tattoos.

In the 1990s, things aren't quite so sexist. Instead, we have the tallest, fastest roller-coaster – for those of us brave enough to give it a go.

Did you know that more than a million ice creams are eaten on the Pleasure Beach every season – along with nearly 48 miles of hot dog sausages? (Presumably by those who *don't* ride on The Big One or the Revolution!)

And that's after our wonderful landladies have fried up half a million eggs for breakfast and two million rashers of bacon – every day.

One of the reasons that Blackpool continues to be successful is that it has kept up with the times. There is always something new to see and do in Blackpool, how ever many times you come here.

One of my earliest memories about Blackpool was its wonderful summer shows, particularly at the Winter Gardens, where I began in the early '70s.

The Evening Gazette also holds a special place in my affections, because it was there that my first astrological columns appeared, in 1979.

Since then, I have travelled all over the world, but must confess I have never found anywhere quite like Blackpool.

This book cannot fail to bring back memories for its readers, whether they, like me, live here – or whether they have visited on holiday.

The pictures might be mainly black and white – but they certainly bring out Blackpool's colourful past. I, for one, feel sure the future will be one to match.

Russell Grant
August 1994

Curtain Up

Blackpool at the turn of the Century

VISITORS to the bustling Blackpool of today find it hard to imagine how things used to be.

As recently as 1800, there was little to Blackpool beyond a few fishermen's cottages and a handful of small hotels.

Yet, from very humble beginnings, Blackpool has grown into Britain's number one holiday resort, a magnet for the young and old alike.

Although there is evidence that the Romans and, indeed, Anglo-Saxon and Danish settlers, moved along the plains of the Fylde, it held little attraction for them - and certainly none of the allures it holds for tourists today!

Indeed, most of the development has been in the last century, coinciding with the growth in the tourism industry. Much of the residential property was built between the wars and, in the space of just 200 years, Blackpool has grown from no more than a small village into one of the most densely populated urban areas outside London.

The word Fylde comes from the Danish "Ffylde" meaning plain, while Blackpool's name is even more literal, referring to what was once a murky black pool on the seashore.

Two streams, one from Marton Mere and one known as Spen Dyke, which brought water from Marton Moss, met at Spen Corner, near the site of Waterloo School. From there, the stream flowed through peaty soils to the sea, collecting in a dark brown pool near what is now Manchester Square - the original black pool.

To the north of the pool, there were cliffs, which rose to a height of about 100ft, near the site of the present North Shore boating pool.

The cliffs then fell away slowly towards Norbreck, with a small 'ginnell' known now as Gynn Square being the only opening in the landscape to break the open view.

Early references to the town can be found as far back as the 15th and 16th century, but it was not until the early 1700s that the first visitors trickled into town - and another 100 years more before the tourism trade really gathered momentum.

As early sketches show, Blackpool has grown quite beyond recognition in a relatively short space of time.

In One Day...

18,649 people hired deckchairs
39 children were lost — and found
2 people were rescued by the Lifeboat
27 people were treated for heat exhaustion
2 people were taken to hospital
60 tons of rubbish were cleaned from the streets and beach
3,048 people went to the Zoo
10 people died suddenly — two of them visitors
57 men were charged with being drunk
122,000 people travelled on the trams
46 people missed their coach home.

Blackpool as it was in 1750 - a handful of hotels perched upon the cliffs.

Even in 1880, the town was still in its infancy. This cart track eventually became Central Drive.

Paddling was already becoming popular among those brave enough to scramble down the rough stone steps to the beach. This sketch, from 1837, shows the beginnings of North Shore.

A decade later, cannons were perched on the cliffs to fend off any potential attack from across the seas.

This thatched cottage and stable stood to the North of the Metropole Hotel site, at the junction of Cocker Street and the Promenade. It was knocked down in 1869.

By 1867, architects were beginning to take an interest in the development of this new North West resort. These elegant hotels – dubbed Regents Terrace and Brighton Parade – were to occupy the land immediately north of Talbot Square.

Elegantly-clad lords and ladies were to be found promenading along North Pier – the first of Blackpool's three – when it opened in 1863. A toll was designed to keep the working classes away.

In 1780, there were still only about 50 houses and a few dusty roads in the town. But the hotel trade was beginning – and you could stay in Blackpool's best hotels for 10d a day. Among these was Bailey's Hotel, built in 1785. Owner Lawrence Bailey charged visitors 3s 4d a night, with 1s for dinner or supper and 8d for breakfast or tea. The hotel is still as popular today – but better known as the Metropole.

One of Blackpool's earliest landlords was a man called Whiteside, who opened a boarding house on the cliffs at North Shore in 1735. Twenty years on, there were four ale-houses in Blackpool and two in Layton and by 1780, there were four principal hotels for the wealthy on the seafront - Bailey's (the Metropole), Forshaws (the Clifton), Hudson's (the old Lewis's site) and Hull's (the old Woolworth site, now Pricebusters).

Names of other early inhabitants still crop up in conversation locally – many reflected in the town's street names.

Edward Tyldesley of Myerscough was one such example. He built a summer hunting lodge – Fox Hall – near to what is now known as Foxhall Square.

The family estate was sold in 1759 and some of the tenants went on to take in summer visitors, serving them with plenty of home cooking and their ever-popular home-brewed ale.

But the visitors who returned to stay in the nearby village of Blackpool in those early years found not the plush hotels and friendly boarding houses of today, but barns and outhouses.

In 1787, John Bonney, whose parents owned the Gynn Inn, opened Bonney's Hotel. Accommodation here was a little cheaper than at Bailey's – but then it did not have the bowling green and bathing house of which Lawrence Bailey was able to boast! Bonney's was demolished in 1902 and the King Edward VII Hotel was later built on the site.

Bathing machines were available for hire from 6.30am for daring sea dippers of the 1880s. A bell was rung several times a day on the beach to warn the male bathers that ladies were coming in. The men had then to leave the water ...and were liable to be fined if they peeped at the bathing beauties! Mr Rishton's machines, pictured here, were opposite the Claremont Hotel.
A paddle was as much as one could take without hiring a bathing machine. Deckchairs were not allowed on the beach until 1914.

READ'S SEA WATER BATHS.—SOUTH BEACH. (Between North and South Piers.)

GENTLEMEN'S SWIMMING BATH.—60 feet by 24 feet. Supplied Daily with 60,000 gallons of Pure, Tepid, Filtered Sea Water, fitted up with every Convenience, and provided with Separate Dressing Rooms. Admission—SIXPENCE each. Bathers may avail themselves of a Cold Shower Bath without additional Charge. LADIES' SWIMMING BATH, 40 feet by 15 feet, is also provided with Separate Dressing Rooms, excellently fitted up, at the same Charge. LADIES' BATHING COSTUMES, 2d. extra. GENTLEMEN'S, 1d. extra.

PRIVATE HOT, COLD, SHOWER, TEPID, AND VAPOUR BATHS.

FIRST CLASS.											SECOND CLASS.									
1 Bath	...	...	...	...	...	1s. 6d.					1 Bath	...	...	...	...	...	...	0s. 9d.
6 Baths	...	...	...	...	...	5s. 0d.					6 Baths	...	...	...	...	...	...	3s. 6d.
12 Baths	...	...	...	...	...	9s. 0d.					12 Baths	...	...	...	...	...	...	6s. 0d.

VAPOUR AND SHOWER BATH ... ... 1s. 6d.   SLIPPER AND SHOWER BATH ... ... 1s. 6d.

THE PRIVATE BATHS are all in Separate Compartments, and for the use of each Bather are re-filled with 100 gallons of Pure, Filtered Sea Water, and Provided with Towels, Flesh Brushes, Combs, &c.

AN INSPECTION OF THE ABOVE ESTABLISHMENT INVITED.

Piped water first came to Blackpool in 1864 and one of the first people to take advantage of it was Jonathan Read, who opened his popular public baths on what was then South Beach.
In the interests of propriety, men and women were again segregated, while two classes of baths were offered. First class would cost you 1s 6d, but second class only half that, at 9d.

Carriages conveyed people from outside the old vicarage on South Promenade to the Winter Gardens and Royal Palace Gardens for the fee of 6d.

Uncle Tom's Cabin, a bawdy singing and dancing house dating from the 1850s, had its own platform for open-air dancing, which was accompanied by a pianist, fiddler and cornet player. When built, on the site of a small snack stall, it stood a good way back from the cliff-face, but as the cliffs were eroded by the elements, it vanished along with them.
The Gynn Estate Company replaced it at the turn of the century with today's version, well away from the fate which claimed its predecessor, on the east side of the road and tramway.

Small fishing boats and pleasure craft pulled up on to the slade on Central Beach well into this century.

St John's Church tower and the Town Hall clock can clearly be picked out on this photograph taken from North Pier jetty in 1890.

Donkeys have been associated with Blackpool almost from day one and certainly figured on early postcards. They are pictured here in 1898 giving rides on the sands in front of the old Palatine Hotel, at the bottom end of Adelaide Street. The site is now occupied by the Coral Island amusement complex.
Picture postcards first went on sale in Blackpool in 1898.
A product of the Edwardian era, when postage was relatively cheap, they were initially slow to catch on. But by 1903, business was booming and the Blackpool Times reported sales of up to 1,000 a day!

The sun did not always shine on Blackpool, as this picture from the turn of the century shows. Ladies were forced to hang on to their hats as the blustery winds whipped up the Irish Sea on Central Promenade.

The Gynn Inn dates from 1745. It was a busy place in Edwardian days, as passengers wishing to travel to Bispham, Fleetwood and Cleveleys had to change trams at the terminus there. This picture, from the turn of the century, shows the tram terminus.

Even in 1921, there was still little development in the surrounding area.

The Gynn Hotel of today was designed by Blackpool architect Halstead Best and opened in 1939.

There has been a waxworks in Blackpool since the mid-19th century. In 1885, it was 2d to visit Madame Tussaud's on Central Promenade. Some say the modern frontage to Louis Tussauds, added at the end of the '70s, detracts from the fine architecture of the adjacent Huntsman building.

Among the first visitors to Blackpool, in 1869, was a certain Mr Charles Dickens. By the turn of the century, everybody who was anybody wanted to visit this new bathing resort.

The Talbot Road laundry grew in response to the burgeoning hotel trade at the turn of the century, providing employment for dozens of local women.

Another turning point came in 1871, with The Bank Holiday Act. This created four additional holidays a year, at Easter, Whitsuntide, late August and at Christmas, encouraging thousands of workers from the inland mill towns to visit Blackpool for the first time. Having sampled it for the day, they invariably wanted to return again for a full week – and so began Blackpool's life as a resort for the working classes.

Three Piers for Blackpool

NORTH PIER, opened in 1863, was Blackpool's first – and longest – pier, measuring 2,130ft, including the jetty.

It was designed to seat between 3,000 and 4,000 people at a time and, in its first year, half a million patrons passed through its gates.

The North Pier has been an integral part of Blackpool's entertainment scene for almost 150 years and, in that time, been visited by people from all over the world.

The project was put forward by the Blackpool Sea Water Company, which supplied hotels in the prestigious Claremont Gardens area, north of the Metropole.

The plan for North Pier was to 'afford greater promenading space of the most invigorating kind'. At first, people were against the idea and said it was tempting providence to build anything in the way of the tide.

The Sea Water Company wanted it to be called Claremont Pier and thought its services should be two-fold. By carrying sea water pipes bearing tidal water to the best hotels, those visitors who had complained they could not always get a bath would be satisfied!

The genteel promenading at the North end would be away from the 'rowdy element' from Lancashire and Yorkshire – hence the introduction of a toll.

The first pile was sunk on June 27, 1862, with the pier opening on May 21 the following year
Thousands came by train from out of town to join in the fun and the local town crier proclaimed the day a general holiday.
It was a day that went with a bang – thanks to the town's only artillery piece, a 12-pounder cannon belonging to the company chairman, Major
Francis Preston. The day also brought Blackpool its first newspaper pictorial publicity – in the London News.

The jetty was added in 1869 and, in 1874, the directors added an acre to the decking and built the Indian Pavilion, pictured here. This was based on the design of a Hindu temple and built on the pier's north wing, while an open-air bandstand was added on the south side.

Boats sailed from the pier to Southport, Barrow and Piel Island.
One of the regular visitors was the Queen of the North, launched in 1895, shortly before this picture was taken. She went on to have a brave career as a minesweeper during the First World War, during which she was torpedoed and sunk.

Sunlight soap, Bovril and Pritchard's teething powders were among household essentials of the day – not to mention a pair of good-fitting corsets!

Tragedy struck when a blaze broke out on the pier in 1921.
People were just heading home for tea, following the afternoon concerts on the pier, on the evening of Sunday, September 21.
Suddenly, a column of smoke rose into the air from the Indian Pavilion. The fire brigade's task was hopeless. Flames were high in the air before firemen could get near the pavilion and in 30 minutes, it was in ashes.
Lost in the fire were valuable instruments and a large library of music but, thankfully, no lives.

History was to repeat itself 17 years later, again on a Sunday afternoon, when a blaze, believed to have been caused by a discarded cigarette end, broke out in the Indian Pavilion.

Blackpool attracts more visitors in a year than Greece and all of the Greek islands.

More than 60 artistes carried on as usual, despite losing £20,000-worth of costumes, instruments and scenery – a lot of money in those days! - in the blaze. Musicians had to play from memory and the showgirls changed into their borrowed costumes in very cramped conditions – but it was 'On with the Show' as usual – as this advertisement promised.

LAWRENCE WRIGHT'S
ON WITH THE SHOW

GOES ON

IN SPITE OF FIRE! AND WILL STILL
BE THE

RAGING SUCCESS
OF BLACKPOOL

2-45 p.m. and 7-45 p.m.

NORTH PIER, BLACKPOOL

TEL. : BLACKPOOL 980.

By now, the pier had become the regular venue for 'On with the Show', a production devised by the late Lawrence Wright, which ran virtually every year on the pier up to the 50s, when Bernard Delfont took over. And never were the words more apt than on June 19, 1938, when the cast did just that!

The new pavilion, which took more than a year to build, was opened in 1939 and proved very art deco in style.

Fire was again to strike North Pier in 1966, not long after the wraps came off a major redevelopment scheme...

....and again in 1974, leading to the demolition of the seaward end of the pier.

Memories are made of this. A typical summer's day on North Pier in 1963, with barely an empty deckchair to be found.

Now where have they gone? Same day, same month – but very different weather was to be found on July 24, 1975.

Millions of pounds have been spent on the piers by owners First Leisure to ensure that they stay an integral part of Blackpool's holiday scene. This two-storey Venetian carousel, brought over from Italy, was installed on the Pier as part of the Victorian revamp of 1991 and cost £500,000. Sporting gondolas as well as horses, it can carry up to 70 people.

Central Pier began its life on May 30, 1868, with the title of South Pier and remained so called for many years. Many of the same entrepreneurs who had been instrumental in building North Pier were again involved. Dancing has always been a feature of the Central Pier and in the 1870s, it was the dancing that attracted the greatest crowds.

Musicians were hired in 1873 at the rate of 10s per man per week for playing from 9.30am to 12, 3-5pm and 7-9pm. Admission to the Pier was 1d and the musicians were allowed to take a collection.

At one time, there were regular steamship sailings from the pier, but these were eventually discontinued and the jetty, which had become costly to maintain, was demolished in the 1920s.

This picture of the pier entrance was taken in 1953.

This aerial shot shows the Central Pier and busy beach scene in the '50s.

Anglers continued to fish off Central Pier's timber jetty, until that too became badly battered by storms. The remaining stumps, pictured here, were finally removed in 1976.

This is how most people picture Central Pier today. All three piers became part of First Leisure's entertainment empire in 1982.

This elegant picture of Victoria, now known as South, Pier was taken soon after it was built in 1893. It continued under that name until 1930 and was classed as the élite of all piers.
People would spend Sunday morning at the fashion parade on North Pier, followed by an afternoon stroll on the Victoria.
Its Grand Pavilion hosted a variety of artistes dating back before the First World War, including Herr Arnold Blome who was a notable figure, along with his orchestra, pre-1914.

Other popular names included the likes of Fred Walmsley, the greatest pierrot of them all, who ran two shows in Blackpool, including The Victorians, at the Grand Pavilion. There would be more than a few eyebrows raised today if this troupe – Carlton's White Coons – took to the stage under the same name.

The resort has 120,000 holiday beds – more than the whole of Portugal.

It was entertainer Harry Korris who suggested the name of the Victoria Pier be changed to South. He pointed out to the then chairman of directors John Hacking that it was ridiculous to have a North and Central Pier, then a Victoria Pier. The logical sequence was to have a South Pier, he said.
"People", he said, "will then know where they are."
Shortly afterwards, the name was changed.

The pier, which is 928ft long and was commandeered by the RAF during the Second World War, was totally destroyed by fire in 1958, but redeveloped, in up-to-the-minute style, by 1963.
In the '60s, entertainment covered everything from the Sooty Show to international wrestling!

Blackpool in Colour

Bang up to date in Blackpool. This is the image visitors to the town get if they come today.

The bird's eye view – the Metropole Hotel as seen from a seagull's perch on the rooftops.

Blackpool's famous pier and beach.

Another bird's eye view, this time of the Winter Gardens.

Above: The magnificent Tower ballroom in all its glory.

Right: Saved – undeniably Matcham's masterpiece. The Grand Theatre.

A less familiar view of Blackpool Pleasure Beach – the sixth most popular tourism attraction in the world.

All the fun of the fair is shown by this aerial shot.

Switch on night in Talbot Square.

The Tower – during the Illuminations.

Blackpool by Light…

The BIG One! The latest addition to the stomach-churning rides on Blackpool Pleasure Beach was built in 1994.

Blackpool Pleasure Beach at night.

Sunset over Central Pier

Blackpool Tower

Mention the name Blackpool and people immediately think of the Tower. Now 100 years old it is, without doubt, the town's most famous landmark.

The project was fathered by Alderman Sir John Bickerstaffe, who, from humble beginnings as a fisherman's son, went on to become Mayor of the town and an Honorary Freeman of the Borough.
Without his business skills, ambition and love for the town of his birth, the scheme would never have got off the ground.
Bickerstaffe's idea for the Tower came after Gustave Eiffel built his particular pinnacle for the Paris exhibition of 1889.
Blackpool's smaller version was built by Heenan and Froude Limited of Worcester and commemorative medals were struck to mark the laying of the foundation stone in 1891.

The seafront site was originally occupied by Dr Cocker's aquarium and menagerie. This picture was taken about 1880, when admission to the attractions was only 6d.

The Daily Graphic of July 25, 1891 carried details of the the share flotation.

The entrance to the aquarium can still be seen as the first struts of steel take shape above.

It was to be a formidable neighbour for residents behind Bank Hey Street as it grew… and grew… and grew!

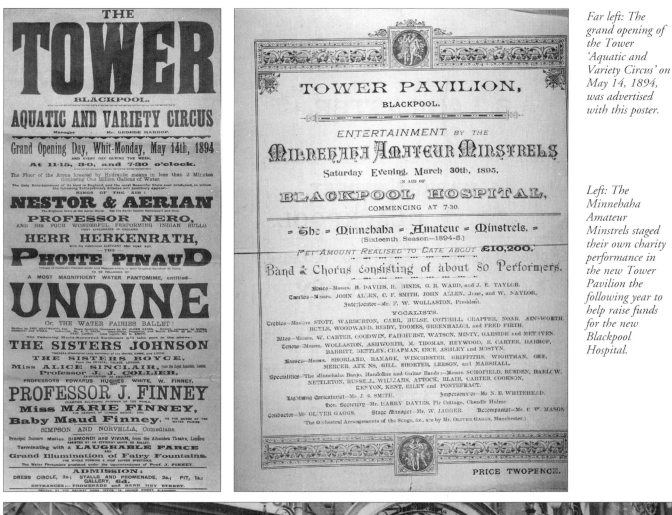

Far left: The grand opening of the Tower 'Aquatic and Variety Circus' on May 14, 1894, was advertised with this poster.

Left: The Minnehaha Amateur Minstrels staged their own charity performance in the new Tower Pavilion the following year to help raise funds for the new Blackpool Hospital.

Newsboys herald the end of the Boer War outside the Tower in May 1902.

The town receives more than £430 million in revenue through the tourism trade.

By 1903, the Tower had its own official programme and guide.

Postcards were quick to cash in on the new attraction.

These were some of the Tower's first employees. These barmaids, pictured in 1898, worked in the Long Bar.

In 1913, a military band played on the Tower Balcony as King George V and Queen Mary honoured the town with a royal visit.

Right and below: The unenviable task of painting the Tower to protect it from the elements is carried out by an army of intrepid workers known as stick men.

This brave chap, pictured in 1953, seemed no more perturbed to be painting 500ft above sea level than he would on terra firma!

The Tower's famous ballroom was virtually destroyed by fire in December 1956. More than £500,000 was spent on its refurbishment with an army of skilled artists and craftsmen employed to restore the magnificent ceiling, with its carved pillars and cherubs, in a task which took more than a year to complete.

The Tower was bedecked in all its glory for the Coronation of 1953, as flags, shields and rosettes were strung across the Promenade for the festivities.

The mighty WurliTzer, which also had to be restored, is pictured here being returned to the ballroom in March 1958.

This was the scene in the Tower ballroom before the re-opening concert in May 1958.

Some feared the Tower might be demolished, during the redevelopment plans for the Blackpool central area in 1976. In fact, it is one of the few parts of this picture which remain intact, the rest having been wiped out to make way for the new Hounds Hill shopping centre.

The Tower has always presented people
with a challenge.

Two Lancashire lads scaled the flagpole
undetected in May 1929 – but protester
John Smith made sure the nation's eyes
were focussed on him when he perched
in the Tower top crow's nest in August
1980.

Smith, a 30-year old loner with a
history of depression, climbed over a
wooden gate to perch himself 480ft up
in the crow's nest., with just two
chocolate bars and a radio for company.
It took police two days of negotiating to
persuade him down. He was later
bound over to keep the peace for two
years – but he didn't. Instead, he went
on to gain further notoriety when he
killed renowned Judge William
Openshaw, at his home near Preston, on
May 12 the following year.

At Smith's trial at Leeds Crown Court
in November 1981, it was revealed he
carried a death list of famous people,
ranging from politicians and police
chiefs to members of the Royal Family.

"Oh, we do like to be beside the seaside!" No visit to Blackpool was complete without hearing Tower organist Reginald Dixon – 'Mr Blackpool'
– belting out his most famous melodies on the mighty WurliTzer.

An unusual visitor to Blackpool came in August 1984 in the shape of King Kong, an 84ft high inflatable gorilla, flown in from San Diego, California, which spent three weeks attached to the Tower!

The Tower was the venue for its first – and last – Tower-top wedding in May 1985, when Karl Bartoni married fiancée Wendy Stokes, in a carriage suspended on a 400ft cable.
Revd John Cayton of St Paul's Church, Whitegate Drive, officiated at the 20-minute ceremony, which was relayed by loudspeakers to the crowds below.
Stuntman Bartoni quipped beforehand: "If anything goes wrong, it will be the shortest marriage on record!"

Left: Abseilers have seen the Tower as a fund-raising challenge since Pat Woods showed the way in 1986. Right: The Tower has also been a popular advertising tool. It was used by Everest double glazing in a campaign after the company double glazed the entire 52 windows in the observatory deck. The Royal Mail added a new twist in 1993, when they turned the Tower into a £ sign. Undoubtedly the most controversial has been the decision to allow an advertising slogan along the entire length of the Tower for the 1994 season.

Right: The Tower has turned up in some unusual forms, too. In solid silver…

…Meccano…(far right).

...and in cake! This one was baked for the re-opening in 1958 and is seen being cut by Douglas Bickerstaffe JP, chairman of the Tower directors, watched by Reginald Dixon.

The Tower frontage has been regularly updated to keep pace with modern trends. This was how it appeared to the visitors of the 1950s.

Not everyone goes up the Tower the conventional way. Rocket man Kinnie Gibson came to Blackpool from New York, in July 1986, shooting himself 85ft up the Tower with the aid of a powered back-pack.

In 1969, it was given a £100,000 face lift with a new 240ft frontage designed by local architects MacKeith Dickinson.

It was revamped again in 1977 and in 1984. The restoration programme begun that year, when the Tower also received Grade I listed building status, revealed once again the murals, tiles and walls which had been covered during the screening of 1977!
The original Victorian look is now back in vogue, following a £14 million transformation scheme started in 1990. The Tower top was painted silver for the Queens' Silver Jubilee in 1977. For the Tower's own centenary in 1994, special planning permission and listed building consent had to be obtained so that the Tower could be painted gold.

The Tower's Vital Statistics:

HEIGHT: 518ft 9ins
WEIGHT: 3478 tons of steel and 352 tons of cast iron
FLAGPOLE: 60ft long
It takes nine tons of paint to cover it and needs 10,000 light bulbs for its Illuminations' dress.

The circus arena is situated between the four main legs of the Tower. The floor can be lowered and the arena filled with 40,000 gallons of water.

The Eiffel Tower, in comparison, is 985 ft tall and contains more than 7,000 tons of steel.

The Winter Gardens

The Winter Gardens were designed by Oldham architect Thomas Mitchell and the formal opening performed in July 1878 by the then Lord Mayor of London, Sir Thomas Owton. With its open-air gardens and skating rink, it enjoyed mixed fortunes until the Opera House, then known as Her Majesty's, was added in 1889.

Her Majesty's Opera House was designed by leading theatrical architect Frank Matcham.
It formed part of the Winter Gardens complex, which went on to become part of the Blackpool Tower Company, but is now owned by First Leisure.

The floral hall in all its splendour early this century.

These men and women were the Opera House staff in 1942.

The Empress Ballroom and Indian Lounge were added in 1896, along with the Big Wheel.
The lounge was demolished in 1964 to make way for what is now the Planet Room.

*This was how the
Winter Gardens were
advertised at the turn
of the century.*

WINTER GARDENS, BLACKPOOL.

General Manager:
Mr. Jno. R. Huddlestone.

This magnificent establishment, unrivalled in the World, comprises a series of
places of Entertainment, all under one roof.   The Buildings cover six acres—
the block consisting of one vast square, with a street on each of the four sides.

THE ENTRANCES.   Church Street, under the Glass
    Dome ; Victoria Street, a magnificent New Crystal
    Palace Entrance, direct from the Promenade ;
    Leopold Grove and Adelaide Street.
GRAND PAVILION OR CONCERT ROOM.
    Licensed for Stage Plays.   Holding capacity about
    12,000.
HER MAJESTY'S OPERA HOUSE.   Holding
    capacity about 2,500.
FLORAL HALL.   180 feet by 42 feet.
FERNERY & PALM HOUSE.   130 feet by 30 feet.
BILLIARD SALOON.   Four Tables.   The hand-
    somest Billiard Room in Europe.
GRILL ROOM.   For Chops, Steaks, &c.
GRAND SALOON.   For Refreshments.

GRAND BUFFET.   For Luncheons, Dinners, &c.
TEMPERANCE SALOON.   For Teas, &c.
INDIAN JUNGLE.   For Shooting at Moving Objects.
EXTENSIVE ILLUMINATED GROUNDS.   Laid
    out in choice Flower Beds and Lawns.
THE GIGANTIC WHEEL.
CONSERVATORIES.   With charming collection of
    Tropical Plants.
THE ITALIAN GARDENS.   With the latest
    Novelty from the Paris Exhibition—"Les Montagnes
    Russes."
THE EMPRESS BALLROOM.   The largest in the
    World.   Parquet Floor laid on 2,000 spiral springs.
THE NEW ORIENTAL LOUNGE.   Eclipsing all
    the Palaces of the East.

The Splendour of these Magnificent Combined Palaces of Amusement
is Unrivalled in the Universe and is the wonder of everyone how   **Admission 6d.**
                much can be seen and heard for the small

*The Olympia
exhibition and
amusement hall
were added in
1928, with the
Spanish Hall,
Baronial Hall,
Renaissance
Room and
Galleon Bar
coming the
following year.*

The present Opera House is the third on the same site and was designed by Blackpool architect Charles MacKeith. It was the largest theatre in the country, seating almost 3,000 people, when it opened. It still boasts the largest stage in Britain.

There are 3,500 hotels, guest houses and self-catering flats in the resort.

The Opera House had the honour of staging the first Royal Variety Show outside London, in 1955.
The Queen and Duke of Edinburgh watched from the specially-built Royal Box.

Stars of the Royal Variety show included George Formby, Alma Cogan, Arthur Askey and Charlie Cairoli. This was the complete line-up.

After the show, they were introduced to the Queen and Prince Philip. Tower organist Reginald Dixon, who performed during the show, is pictured meeting the Queen.

This aerial view of the Winter Gardens was taken in the '30s.
The area west of Coronation Street had much in common with its televised Manchester namesake in those days! Note the advent of 'talkies'
being advertised on the Olympia building entrance.

1889 BLACKPOOL OPERA HOUSE 1989

THIS COMMEMORATIVE 'ROLL OF HONOUR' WAS UNVEILED JULY 26TH 1989 BY
LORD BERNARD DELFONT TO MARK THE CENTENARY OF THE BLACKPOOL OPERA HOUSE

1889 WILSON BARRETT	1914 EDWARD COMPTON	1939 GEORGE FORMBY	1964 ROSEMARY SQUIRES	1987 THE NOLANS
1890 BRINSLEY SHERIDAN	1915 CICELY COURTNEIDGE	1940 ARTHUR ASKEY	1965 STAN STENNETT & THE	1988 LES DAWSON
1891 OSMOND TEARLE	1916 NEIL MASKELYNE	1941 FRANK RANDLE	BLACK & WHITE MINSTREL SHOW	1989 MARTI WEBB AND CATS
1892 CHARLES WYNDHAM	1917 SEYMOUR HICKS	1942 WEBSTER BOOTH & ANNE ZIEGLER	1966 THE BLUEBELL GIRLS	1990
1893 KATE VAUGHAN	1918 SIR THOMAS BEECHAM	1943 WILFRED PICKLES	1967 BRUCE FORSYTH	1991
1894 C. AUBREY SMITH	1919 ROBERTSON HARE	1944 SID FIELD	1968 TESSIE O'SHEA	1992
1895 EMMA HUTCHISON	1920 PHYLLIS NEILSON-TERRY	1945 JIMMY JEWEL & BEN WARRISS	1969 VAL DOONICAN	1993
1896 WEEDON GROSSMITH	1921 FRANK FORBES-ROBERTSON	1946 JOSEF LOCKE	1970 THE BACHELORS	1994
1897 AGNES HEWITT	1922 MRS PATRICK CAMPBELL	1947 DAVE MORRIS	1971 RUDY HORN	1995
1898 MARIE STUDHOLME	1923 BRANSBY WILLIAMS	1948 CHARLIE CHESTER	1972 CILLA BLACK	1996
1899 ADA BLANCHE	1924 EDNA BEST	1949 ARTHUR HAYNES	1973 DANNY LA RUE	1997
1900 ADA REEVE	1925 RAYMOND HUNTLEY	1950 NAT JACKLEY	1974 NORMAN VAUGHAN	1998
1901 LILY LANGTRY	1926 JESSIE MATTHEWS	1951 VERA LYNN	1975 FREDDIE STARR	1999
1902 JULIA NEILSON	1927 EVELYN LAYE	1952 TERRY THOMAS	1976 DON MACLEAN & THE	2000
1903 AMY McNEIL	1928 WILFRED HYDE-WHITE	1953 HARRY SECOMBE	BLACK & WHITE MINSTREL SHOW	2001
1904 CHARLES CHAPLIN	1929 PEGGY ASHCROFT	1954 TONY HANCOCK	1977 DAWSON CHANCE	2002
1905 VICTOR ANDRE	1930 SIR JOHN BARBIROLLI	1955 ALMA COGAN	1978 TOM O'CONNOR	2003
1906 ELLALINE TERRISS	1931 GRACIE FIELDS	1956 EVE BOSWELL	1979 FRANK CARSON	2004
1907 ALBERT CHEVALIER	1932 CARL BRISSON	1957 YANA	1980 MIKE YARWOOD	2005
1908 JAMES FORBES-ROBERTSON	1933 GEORGE CLARKE	1958 DAVID WHITFIELD	1981 KEN DODD	2006
1909 PERCY HUTCHISON	1934 BILLY BENNETT	1959 JILL DAY	1982 SYD LITTLE & EDDIE LARGE	2007
1910 ANNIE HUGHES	1935 ALBERT BURDON	1960 TOMMY STEELE	1983 PAUL DANIELS	2008
1911 EVELYN MILLARD	1936 RANDOLPH SUTTON	1961 SHIRLEY BASSEY	1984 RUTH MADOC & HI DE HI	2009
1912 ANNA PAVLOVA	1937 FRED SANBORN	1962 EDDIE CALVERT	1985 TOMMY CANNON & BOBBY BALL	2010
1913 FRED TERRY	1938 STANLEY HOLLOWAY	1963 JIMMY EDWARDS	1986 GRACE KENNEDY	2011

This roll of honour, depicting a century of stars, was unveiled in 1989 by Lord Bernard Delfont.

Building began on the Big Wheel in 1895, when the Winter Gardens Company decided they needed something to combat the growing magnetism of the Tower.
It was copied from the American Ferris Wheel, built for the Chicago World Fair in 1893, and was opened to the public in 1896.
A total of 250 men started work on 1,000 tons of steel. It took a year to build, was 220ft high and huge cables turned the contraption on an axle that itself weighed 30 tons. It was the biggest in the world.

There were 30 carriages, each capable of carrying up to 30 people and more than 4,000 people queued for their first ride when it opened in August 1896, charging the princely sum of 3d a trip.
A revolution took between 15 and 20 minutes and operators boasted you could view five countries from the top on a clear day!

The Big Wheel and Tower gave Blackpool an unmistakable skyline in the 1920s.

By 1929, things had gone full circle. The Big Wheel was on its way down for good, as property turned to rubble in nearby Talbot Road. The Wheel was deemed a loss-maker and dismantled when the Tower Company took over the Winter Gardens.
A scrap dealer by the name of Eli Ward and his family, from Eccles, were the last passengers to ride the wheel on October 20, 1928. Carriages were sold off at £20 each.

The Victoria Street entrance to the Winter Gardens as it was in 1885.

First Leisure, which now owns both the Tower and Winter Gardens, decided to revive the Wheel idea with their new Big Wheel, which opened on Central Pier in 1990.

Costing £750,000 to build, the Dutch-built wheel is 108ft high and has 216 seats. The pier had to be reinforced before the wheel could be erected.

All Change

Blackpool's motto is Progress – and by the turn of the century, the march was certainly on.
Yet, the rural community was still thriving, if you strayed far enough away from the seafront.

This cottage store was typical of the many which supplied families in Blackpool at the turn of the century.

There has been a windmill at Marton for more than 200 years.
What is now Preston New Road was originally Mill Lane and the gable end of the adjacent bowling green buildings carried an advert for the
'halfway house' of the Oxford Hotel.

Two views of rural Marton Moss.

New House Farm, with its corrugated roof, stood at the corner of Snow Lane, later renamed Cherry Tree Road, on the site now occupied by the Evening Gazette building. The farm was 300 years old when it was demolished in 1929 to allow for the widening of Preston New Road.

Layton Road, with its whitewashed cottages, pictured early this century.

It seems they had road works in Layton as long ago as 1925! This view shows the junction of Westcliffe Drive and what was then Poulton New Road.

This was St Joseph's Road, Layton, in 1962. It is now better known as Queenstown and houses Blackpool's only high-rise blocks of flats.

Plans to run trams along Westcliffe Drive to Bispham were thrown out in 1925. This picture, of Westcliffe Drive, shows the old Layton Workingmen's Institute in the foreground, on the right.

Bispham Village was a world apart from Blackpool. This photograph, taken in 1928, shows the old Post Office on what was Church Road. This was later renamed Old Hallows Road. The road to the left is Red Bank Road.

The benefits of Blackpool's bracing sea breezes had already gained a name for themselves in medical circles. Plans were drawn up in 1927 by the Lancashire and Cheshire Miners' Welfare Committee for a convalescent home which would serve hundreds of mineworkers affected by breathing complaints and chest complications arising from work in the region's underground mine shafts. The miner's home is still in service today.

This was the Promenade end of Red Bank Road in 1928. The bank building is still standing today, although the tram terminus has long since disappeared.

On the seafront, across from the Miners' Convalescent Home, the cliffs continued to be seriously eroded by the elements.

Closer to the town centre, the council spent thousands of pounds building Princess Parade, officially opened by Princess Louise in 1912.

The Raikes Smithy was the oldest building in Blackpool until it was destroyed by fire on Christmas Day 1988 and had to be demolished. The Smithy had stood on the site, in Church Street, for more than three centuries and seen the magnificent development at Raikes Hall Park, Gardens and Aquarium.

Raikes Hall was built in the early 19th century. The pleasure gardens and entertainment centre, opened in 1871, covered more than 40 acres of the estate, and were once described as bigger, brighter and better than the world-famous Tivoli Gardens in Copenhagen.
The amusement park was bounded by Park Road, Hornby Road, Whitegate Drive and Raikes Road (now Church Street) and had a veritable army of gardeners employed to keep its flower beds and terraces in pristine condition.

The park contained everything imaginable, from a conservatory and cricket pitch, to a miniature railway and monkey house. There was a skating rink, aviary, boating lake, fireworks and facilities for dancing both indoors and out. This was the entrance to the monkey house.

*By the turn of the century, many of Blackpool's other attractions had begun to take shape, closer to the sea, pulling the crowds away from the
Raikes Hall Estate. These statues were some of the last remnants of the park, pictured before their removal in the '50s.
The park's swan-song was the unsuccessful World Fair of 1901, when it was suggested that the council take over the estate, but the deal was
considered too costly.*

The only reminder of its bygone days is the Raikes Hall pub, on the corner of Liverpool Road and Leamington Road.

The First World War is but a memory now for those senior citizens in Blackpool who were alive in the war years. 1914-1918. Blackpool and Fylde's great Tank Week of 1918 raised an amazing £1.12 million. This was one of the tanks from the First World War pictured in the unmistakable setting of Talbot Square, with Yates' Wine Lodge in the background.

These children were pictured on July Peace Day in 1919.

One of Blackpool's first independent
schools to open was Arnold, in 1896.
The school cadet corps was started four
years later.
Sgt J.F.Burge, Colour Sgt E.Evans and
Sgt W.F.Pilkington were pictured in
1905. Pilkington and Evans both lost
their lives in the First World War.

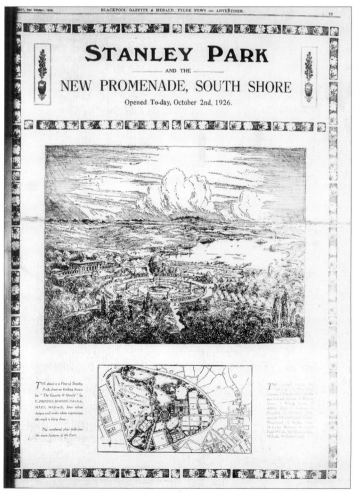

Stanley Park was opened in
October 1926, by the 17th Earl
of Derby. The town's population
that year was 80,730.
The ornamental gardens, lake
and bandstand remain little
changed to this day, although the
nurseries have now been removed
to make way for an indoor sports
hall.

Crowds regularly gathered to listen to the band in the '30s.

This was North Promenade in 1927 – 12 years before the Derby Baths were opened on the site.

Above, below and opposite page, top: The civic fathers paid tribute to the then Lord Derby, by naming the town's new Olympic-sized swimming pool after him.
Derby Baths cost £270,000 to build but the outbreak of war meant Lord Derby was unable to perform the opening ceremony in May 1940, as planned. However, his grandson was able to do the honours when the neighbouring sauna centre opened in 1965. The loss-making baths' complex was demolished amid much controversy in 1990.

1923 saw the first Blackpool Carnival. It was a chance for the local people to let their hair down and have fun.

It was also the year that the South Shore Open Air Baths, built at a cost of £70,000, were officially opened.
Blackpool was fast becoming THE place to be – and more than two million visitors poured into the town in one week alone.

At North Shore, for visitors' enjoyment, there was the boating pool and lift, conveying folk from the clifftop to the beach.

Blackpool's seven miles of unspoilt sands have long been an attraction for children and the bucket and spade brigade still arrives every summer, without fail. These two girls were captured on camera in the 1920s.

In 1938, work began on the new Winter Gardens for South Promenade. The name was later changed to the Harrowside Sun Parlours.

These cottages in Church Street had been standing more than 250 years when they were knocked down to make way for a petrol station in 1937.

Likewise, Stoneyhill Farm in South Shore. The farm, over 300 years old, was demolished in the '30s to allow the building of what is now Albany Avenue.

As time marched on, so did the developers.
By the '20s and '30s, the changes which had made such a dramatic impact to the seafront were beginning to leave their mark on the rest of the town.
Demolition work was rife, as property was flattened to allow road widening schemes and the building of more modern offices and shops. It was an era when much of old Blackpool vanished for ever.

These cottages, in Watson Road, South Shore, were pulled down in 1927.

Talbot Square was widened in 1928, to accommodate increasing numbers of motor cars and charabancs.

Stanley Terrace, on Church Street, at the junction of Caunce Street, was taken down in 1934 as part of a road widening scheme and later replaced by the art deco style block, still known today as Stanley Buildings.

This picture was taken in 1954, when trams still ran along Church Street.

Some of Blackpool's most prestigious homes were on Whitegate Drive. This view of its shops, looking South with the Saddle Inn at the end, on the left, was taken in 1952.

Looking north along Dickson Road in the '30s.

A typical wet winter's day in January 1939. This was the seaward end of Church Street.

Although the traffic may be busier and the vehicles more modern nowadays, the junction at the Oxford looks little different from this today. Yet this picture was taken almost 60 years ago, in 1935.

Blackpool assuming a rare Siberian look. The Orient Café was at the corner of Corporation Street and West Street, where the council offices, once a Boots' chemist, are now. A multi-storey car-park occupies the land to the left, where the horse and cart are pictured.

Three views of Market
Street. Above: In 1939 –
when it still had a
Market Hotel and
Market Hall.

Centre: The open air
market took place on the
site now occupied by BhS.
This was July 1940.

Below: Hymans, Leonard
Dews and H Samuel
were already established
in the area by the late
'50s.

This aerial shot, taken in 1957, shows work already starting on BhS and the West Street multi-storey car-park. Notice that the Palace Theatre is still standing on the site where Lewis' was later built.

Parking was as much of a problem in Birley Street in 1939 as it is today!

Remember the days when you could drive – or catch a bus – along Church Street? This was 1953.

A view over the rooftops from the Metropole Hotel in the mid-20s, showing the Town Hall, Winter Gardens and Big Wheel, Opera House and St John's Parish Church.

The traffic seemed to drive on both the left and the right in 1934…and just look at those crowds!

One of the biggest land deals of the day involved clearing land close to Central Station. This corner plot, fronting Bank Hey Street and Albert Road, was later developed by Marks and Spencer. A McDonald's restaurant now occupies the site.

Red Lees, which stood at the corner of Hornby Road and Park Road, was considered one of the most beautiful homes in Blackpool in its day. It was for many years the home of the late Alderman Joseph Heap, JP, the leader of the local Liberal party and mayor of the town in 1898. Prior to its demolition in 1938, to make way for offices for the Fylde Water Board, it had been the Sunbeam Home for the Blind.

The Bonny Street of today, with its high-rise concrete police station and court complex, bears little resemblance to the narrow alleys and back streets of the '30s. Cottages and cobbled streets were then still a stone's throw from the seafront in Pleasant View.

People were still living in the heart of what is now Blackpool's shopping centre in the '20s and '30s.

Another picture of Bonny Street in the 1930s.

These cottages, in Victoria Street, were demolished when the Gazette and Herald *expanded its original town centre offices. Note the billboards advertising shows at the Tivoli and Feldman's.*

A '50s classic. The Tower pictured from Adelaide Street.

The Three Graces have watched patiently over the corner of Church Street and Temple Street for more than 130 years. They were almost lost during building renovations in 1987 but were saved at the 11th hour to watch over a new Pizzaland restaurant on the site.

Talbot Square still houses the 'new' Town Hall, completed in 1900 and Yates' Wine Lodge, built as the Theatre Royal in 1868, as well as the Clifton Hotel, to the right of this picture.
The 66ft Town Hall spire was removed in 1966, for fear that high winds may blow it down!
Note also the absence of the elegant drinking fountain, which once took pride of place in the centre of Talbot Square. This was removed and replaced with a bus shelter and, later still, public conveniences.

The Palatine Hotel was demolished in 1973, along with the New Inn, to make way for the Palatine and Coral Island amusement centres.

The ex-rector of Stiffkey joined the tattooed lady and the starving bride in Promenade peepshows during the '30s.

Even then, there were half-price bargains to be had in Church Street.

Blackpool's Golden Mile has always been a magnet for artistes sporting the unusual.

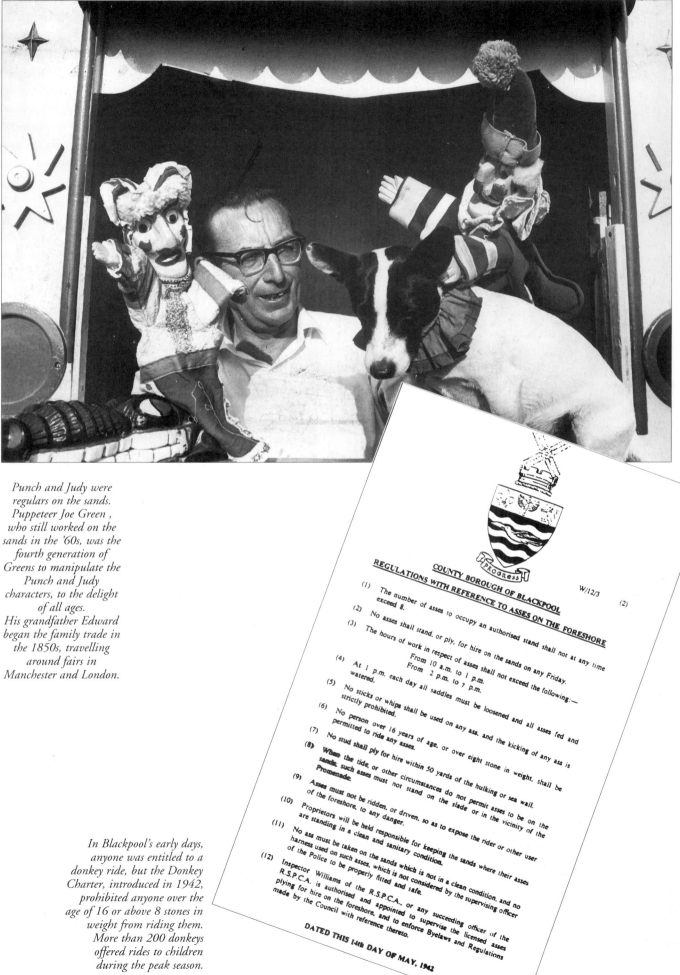

Punch and Judy were regulars on the sands. Puppeteer Joe Green , who still worked on the sands in the '60s, was the fourth generation of Greens to manipulate the Punch and Judy characters, to the delight of all ages. His grandfather Edward began the family trade in the 1850s, travelling around fairs in Manchester and London.

In Blackpool's early days, anyone was entitled to a donkey ride, but the Donkey Charter, introduced in 1942, prohibited anyone over the age of 16 or above 8 stones in weight from riding them. More than 200 donkeys offered rides to children during the peak season.

COUNTY BOROUGH OF BLACKPOOL   W/12/3

REGULATIONS WITH REFERENCE TO ASSES ON THE FORESHORE

(1)   The number of asses to occupy an authorised stand shall not at any time exceed 8.

(2)   No asses shall stand, or ply, for hire on the sands on any Friday.

(3)   The hours of work in respect of asses shall not exceed the following:—

          From 10 a.m. to 1 p.m.
          From 2 p.m. to 7 p.m.

(4)   At 1 p.m. each day all saddles must be loosened and all asses fed and watered.

(5)   No sticks or whips shall be used on any ass, and the kicking of any ass is strictly prohibited.

(6)   No person over 16 years of age, or over eight stone in weight, shall be permitted to ride any asses.

(7)   No stud shall ply for hire within 50 yards of the hulking or sea wall.

(8)   When the tide, or other circumstances do not permit asses to be on the sands, such asses must not stand on the slade or in the vicinity of the Promenade.

(9)   Asses must not be ridden, or driven, so as to expose the rider or other user of the foreshore, to any danger.

(10) Proprietors will be held responsible for keeping the sands where their asses are standing in a clean and sanitary condition.

(11) No ass must be taken on the sands which is not in a clean condition, and no harness used on such asses, which is not considered by the supervising officer of the Police to be properly fitted and safe.

(12) Inspector Williams of the R.S.P.C.A., or any succeeding officer of the R.S.P.C.A. is authorised and appointed to supervise the licensed asses plying for hire on the foreshore, and to enforce Byelaws and Regulations made by the Council with reference thereto.

DATED THIS 14th DAY OF MAY, 1942

One of Blackpool's most infrequent visitors is snow, but this was the view on the seafront in the early '60s.

It was so cold in March 1955 that the sandhills at Clifton Drive froze over, enabling families to practice ice skating in the great outdoors!

On With the Show

Feldman's at the western end of Hounds Hill, started life as the Borough Theatre in September 1877, only two weeks after the nearby Prince of Wales. Music-hall artistes of the day clamoured to play at Feldman's, renamed after music publisher Bertram Feldman.
Mr Feldman also acquired the nearby Bannister's Borough Bazaar, in Bank Hey Street, from the Bannister Brothers, for the sum of £70,000 in 1925 which too was converted into a theatre in 1935.

In the '30s, a summer was not complete without a dose of 'Rockin' the Town' - the Feldman's Summer Show.
Feldman's underwent a £10,000 renovation in April 1938 when all the latest art deco features were introduced. It became a venue for ambitious revues and was one of the first theatres in the country to boast the latest in a steel and asbestos safety curtain!
The theatre could seat 1,680 people and had three bars. Many famous music-hall artistes performed there including Frank Randle.

Feldman's was sold and changed its name to the Queens in 1952, but is still nostalgically recalled by thousands of residents and visitors who remember its place, now occupied by the C&A fashion store.

PRINCE OF WALES THEATRE – later the ALHAMBRA – then the PALACE THEATRE

The Prince of Wales Theatre stood on the Central Promenade site latterly occupied by Lewis's. It cost more than £11,000 to build and was elegant in both design and decor. It was able to accommodate 1,100 people and opened its doors in August 1877 when it also incorporated a public swimming bath. However, its success was short-lived and it was demolished in 1899 to make way for the Alhambra, later re-named the Palace. This photograph was taken in 1896.

Many music-hall greats appeared at the Palace, where its ballroom was popular as far back as the Charleston days. This picture shows the Palace in the 1950s.

The old Palace Band early this century.

Flappers were thrilled with the splendour of the Palace Ballroom.

The theatre was bought by the Blackpool Tower Company, which was absorbed into First Leisure, but sold in 1962 and demolished to make way for the familiar honeycomb façade of Lewis's. This too has since gone, with a new Woolworth's store opening on site in 1994.

THE HIPPODROME

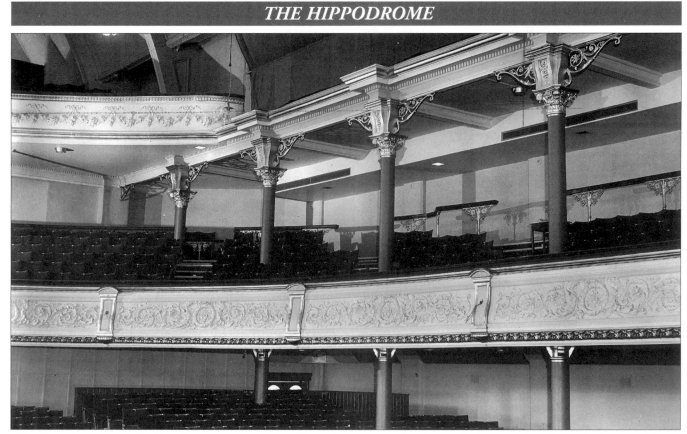

The Hippodrome was on the Church Street site now occupied by MGM cinemas. This photograph shows its splendid carved columns and friezes in 1954.

The Hippodrome was demolished here in 1962 to make way for the ABC, which opened a year later. With a 2,000-seat capacity, it promised facilities to stage the most ambitious of live shows, including West End musicals, and sported a 14ft revolving circular platform as part of the stage.

The ABC cost £300,000 to build and opened in April 1963, with Cliff Richard and the Shadows playing the first summer season.

THE THEATRE ROYAL

The Theatre Royal was built in Clifton Street in 1860 and first known as the Assembly Rooms.
The building was sold at auction to Yates' (of Wine Lodge fame) in 1896, when this picture was taken.

There are 17 million annual visits made to Blackpool.

This was how the auction was advertised in April 1896.

BLACKPOOL, Lancashire.

TO CAPITALISTS, SYNDICATES, BREWERS, TRADESMEN, and OTHERS.

To be Sold by Auction,

BY

JOHN MARSDEN,

ON THE PREMISES (late Free Library),

On WEDNESDAY, the 8th day of April, 1896,

At 3-0 o'clock in the Afternoon,

Subject to the Public Sale Conditions of the Blackpool, Fleetwood, and Fylde District Law Society, and to such other conditions as will be then and there produced,

All that VALUABLE FREEHOLD PROPERTY

Situate in Talbot Square, Talbot Road, and Clifton Street, Blackpool, known as the Theatre Royal Buildings, and comprising the

THEATRE ROYAL

THE FULLY

LICENSED HOTEL,

RESTAURANT, SHOPS, CELLARAGE,

and other Premises.

Any further particulars may be obtained from the AUCTIONEER, 6, Queen's Square, Blackpool; Mr. THOMAS BLANE, Chartered Accountant, Central Beach, Blackpool; Mr. R. B. MATHER, Architect, Lytham Street, Blackpool; or

H. P. MAY, SOLICITOR,

In 1907, it was turned into a cinema and assumed the Tivoli title. With a capacity to seat 1,000 people, it was popular with local people as well as the visitors who saw many an early film played there.

This was the interior in 1934.

The Tivoli was totally renovated in 1951, but a fire was to cause £10,000-worth of damage in the mid-60s, leading to yet another major overhaul. The box-office smash Mary Poppins was the first film to be shown when it re-opened in April 1965. It later served as a bingo hall, a pool hall and cabaret room. It is best known among young people today as Addison's night club.

THE GRAND THEATRE

The Grand Theatre, opened in 1894, is probably Blackpool's best-known theatre today. Yet the architectural masterpiece came close to meeting the same fate as Feldman's and the Palace.

Often called Matcham's masterpiece, the Grand was built in 1894, when the prolific architect also completed the Tower Ballroom and five other theatres around the country.

A plan to demolish the theatre first reared its ugly head in the summer of 1972.

A campaign, launched by theatre-goers who later became known as the Friends of the Grand, caused sufficient concern to force a public inquiry, at which the Theatre won a reprieve.

By then, the Theatre had become a Grade 2 listed building.

But the theatre failed to re-open and became increasingly derelict. It did open in 1977 – but as a Bingo Hall.

It was impresario Thomas Sergenson who hired architect Frank Matcham to create the 'best, prettiest and cosiest theatre possible' Sergenson purchased a block of old cottages and shops on the corner of Church Street and St Ann Street, later renamed Corporation Street in 1887. His plans was to build the Grand Theatre and five shops, the income from which was designed to subsidise the theatre. He put his plans on ice when Matcham was called in to design the Opera House and proceeded with only the shops. In the meantime, he put the site to use by staging a circus on it, housed in a temporary wood and corrugated iron building.

The Friends succeeded in raising the necessary funds, with the help of the council, the Arts Council and Lancashire County Council, to purchase the Theatre from owners EMI in September 1980.

The late, great, comic Les Dawson, who lived for most of his life on the Fylde, was a regular at the Grand. He was topping the bill there in 1984, in 'Laugh with Les' and so was the obvious choice, along with his Roly Poly dancers, to help the Grand celebrate its 90th birthday.

This view, from outside the Grand, was in 1951, when The Blue Lamp, starring Jack Warner, Peter Byrne and Warren Mitchell was playing. Every performance, twice nightly, was packed. The show went on to become the basis for the long-running '60s TV series Dixon of Dock Green.

It re-opened to the public on March 23, 1981, with the Old Vic playing the Merchant of Venice. Starring Prunella Scales and Timothy West. The House Full signs were up – a sign of the times to come.

One of the first major coups for the theatre after its re-opening was a Royal Variety Performance, attended by Prince Charles, on Friday, May 29, 1981.

Most of today's top names started with a season in Blackpool.

The Waterloo Cinema was built pre-1920. It merged with the Palladium in Waterloo Road and was taken over by the South Shore Theatre Company in 1928.
London and Northern Properties of Newcastle converted the old cinema into shops and offices after it was sold in 1960.

Blackpool's Pleasure Beach

Possibly Britain's most popular fun park, this has been owned and managed by three generations of the same family since 1896. It was founded by William George Bean who wanted to create an amusement park where adults could once more play like children.

Among the earliest attractions was Sir Hiram Maxim's Captive Flying Machine which opened to the public on August Bank Holiday Monday 1904 – and is still popular with visitors 90 years on! It was restored and re-painted in its original colours in 1975. This and the helter-skelter were the two most prominent – and popular – attractions in South Shore.

This included the House of Nonsense, Scenic Railway, Grand National, Pleasure Beach Express and River Caves.

What was to become the Pleasure Beach's first Casino building was built as a restaurant and theatre on the sands in 1919. This glorious building was demolished in 1937, not without difficulty. Explosives had to be used to remove some of its solid concrete walls!

The Casino building.

Work had already begun on the new casino by August 1938. Look at the angular animals on the early Noah's Ark.

The new casino building was opened in May 1939 by Lord Stamp, President of the LMS Railway. It still exists, housing the panoramic White Tower restaurant on the first floor. A scenic elevator has also been added, while the casino is now better known as the Horseshoe Showbar.

The Ice Drome was built in 1937. Mr Funshine, the current Pleasure Beach mascot, was in his infancy – on the poster!

The Big Dipper has thrilled generations of visitors to the Pleasure Beach.

Water has also played its part. This was the early water chute in the '30s.

The Big Wheel and Noah's Ark were already proving popular with the bank holiday crowds of 1946.

One of the big thrills in 1937 was a whirl on the Reel.

War had already broken out by March 1940, when this photograph was taken, but people were still prepared to enjoy themselves.

This aerial view of the Pleasure Beach in 1946 shows there were already a good number of attractions. Later years saw the addition of such delights as the mono-rail (1960), the Revolution (1979) and the Avalanche (1988).

Trains and Boats and Planes ...and Trams

Blackpool was fairly inaccessible before the 18th century and it was only after the opening of the first rail link to the Fylde that its popularity as a holiday resort really began to blossom.

Two of the area's principal landowners, Sir Henry Houghton and Thomas Clifton were responsible for laying the first main road into town in 1781, when they crossed the salt marshes from Ashton, on the outskirts of Preston, to Clifton.

It was not long before a stagecoach began plying its trade between Manchester and Blackpool in the summer months. But visitors had to be patient. It took six hours to travel from Preston to Blackpool – and an incredible two days to get to the resort from Yorkshire!

1840 was a real turning point, when the railway came to Poulton-le-Fylde.

Every sort of horse-drawn vehicle Blackpool could muster met the day-trip trains and, for the first time, the resort became within the reach of ordinary Lancashire people.

However, one clergyman did accuse the railways of carrying people 'swiftly and safely to Hell'.

A branch line from Poulton to Blackpool was opened on April 29, 1846 and the resort soon proved to be more popular than neighbouring Fleetwood, which had been reaping the benefit of day trippers by train for some six years.

The first Blackpool terminus was sited in Talbot Road. In 1848, an excursion from O'dham cost 1s for ladies and 1s 6d for gentlemen.
However, the concession had to be withdrawn, as it was suspected the men were masquerading as women in order to get a cheaper fare!
The station was pulled down in 1896.

The first North Station was built in Dickson Road to cater for the thousands of travellers who poured into Blackpool for the tradesmen's holidays.

It remained on that site, little altered, for 70 years, but was demolished in the mid-70s to make way for a supermarket.

Buses poured into the Talbot Mews traffic park in 1932 to convey passengers from the station to the attractions of the seafront and Pleasure Beach.

The present Blackpool North station, a sight familiar to hundreds of today's holidaymakers, was officially opened on April 8, 1974.

The Sands Express was one train NOT to be found at Blackpool North! The engine known as Annie plied her trade along the Promenade, carrying sand from South Shore during the extension and widening of the Promenade in 1905.

The Lancashire and
Yorkshire Railway
advertised Sunday sea
bathing trips to
Fleetwood and Blackpool.
By this time, the fares
had risen to 3s for men
and 1s 6d for women
and children.
Note the small print,
which attempted to
placate the opponents of
Sunday excursions.
'Parties availing
themselves of these trains
will be enabled to bathe
and refresh themselves in
ample time to attend a
Place of Worship.'

Hundreds of visitors poured off the trains at Blackpool Central Station to avail themselves of the facility.

Central Station was much used by trippers during the Wakes' Weeks of the Fifties.

This scene was typical. It shows a factory outing from Oldham arriving at Blackpool Central, in the days when 10-coach trains were the norm.

This aerial view of Central Station in the 1950s shows the former gas works in the background. The railway hostel, to the top left of the picture, owned by the council, was at one time destined to be a YMCA. Some locals still refer to it as the Armistice Buildings and King Edward Buildings, even though its uses have been as diverse as holiday flats and a succession of night clubs.

Central Station closed in 1964. By the time this same picture was taken in July 1971, cars had already taken over much of the land previously occupied by the railway lines. The new Law Courts can be seen at the top right, but not yet the towering police station. Immediately behind the station building, which was used as a bingo hall up to its demolition in 1973, can be seen an arena which was the site of a short-lived outdoor Dolphin Show.

These two arches and canopy were all that stood testimony to the age of steam by January 1974.

By 1977, heavy plant was back on site, developing the £4 million Coral amusement complex. Notice how little altered are the buildings behind the site, on Central Drive.

Although Blackpool never made a name for itself as a port, unlike its smaller neighbour of Fleetwood, boats were not uncommon at the turn of the century, when visitors were able to enjoy pleasure cruises, which set out from the piers to a variety of locations.
This photograph, taken in the 1890s, shows the horse-drawn carriages which conveyed ladies and gentlemen to the North Pier, to catch the steamboat.

The most famous shipwreck in Blackpool was that of Nelson's flagship the Foudroyant. The 2,055-ton ship, which spent a century in naval service, was taken out of active service in 1891 and had become an exhibition vessel.

She was moored off Blackpool when a freak storm whipped up on June 16, 1897, causing her to break her moorings and crash on to the beaches at North Shore. Her 20 crew members were saved and many local people still have souvenirs today which were pulled from the wreckage.

Blackpool was the cradle of British aviation, although calls to have its Squires Gate airport upgraded to international standard have fallen largely on deaf ears.

The first officially recognised aviation meeting in the country was held on the site of the Squires Gate airport in 1909, six years after the Wright Brothers' first flight and a few months after Louis Bleriot crossed the channel for the first time.
It was organised by the Lancashire Aero Club and this photograph of the grandstand shows Mr J. Talbot Clifton of Lytham Hall standing behind the Club's honorary secretary, Colonel Grantham. Members of Lord Lonsdale's private band are gathered to the right of the picture. The air display attracted 200,000 people, but a similar event, planned the following year, proved to be a flop.

The land was used as a racecourse for a time up to the start of the First World War, when it became a sea of huts containing convalescing casualties.

This was the King's Lancashire Military Hospital, on the site of the present aerodrome, in 1915. In May 1919, the first Manchester-Blackpool flight took place, with four Avro bi-planes landing on the sand south of South Pier. More than 30,000 people gathered on the beach to witness the event. Three of the four planes made the journey in 35 minutes – the fourth did it in 25!

Pioneer flier A.V.Roe, the man behind Avro, started the first pleasure flights from the beach at Blackpool, charging five shillings (25p) a time.

Blackpool Council hired Sir Alan Cobham, who entertained the crowds with his flying circus, to survey the resort for a municipal aerodrome. The result was the Stanley Park Field, now the site of the town's zoo, which contained the remains of its old hangars until quite recently. This hangar was newly-built when it was photographed in 1930.

The Mayor and council officials were pictured on a visit to the park airfield in 1928, when they inspected one of the first Imperial Airways planes to arrive from London.

This photograph, taken in 1937, shows passengers queueing up for the pleasure flights.

Above: The RAF Coastal Command trained there and fighter planes flew from Squires Gate in defence of Merseyside during the blitz. These were the first members of the Royal Air Force unit to arrive, in April 1939.

Private enterprise moved on to the Squires Gate site, with flights to the Isle of Man, and there was conflict between the two sites until the outbreak of the Second World War in 1939.

After September of that year, Stanley Park aerodrome became a parachute training centre and was never used for flying again.

By then, Blackpool Corporation had bought Squires Gate from the Clifton estate for £175,000 and planes were happily landing and taking off from the grass.

However, when the Government requisitioned it for a wartime role, proper runway surfaces were laid and the site eventually swelled from 150 acres to 300.

Right: New hangars began to be built there a few weeks later, for the use of the Auxiliary Air Force.

Between 1941 and 1945, Vickers built 4,000 Wellington bombers on the site, while Hawker built 400 Hunter jets there in the peacetime years between 1953 and 1958.

The new airport control tower, with up-to-the-minute technology, was opened in March 1956, replacing the outdated facilities.

The airport was privatised in 1987, but the council still holds all the shares.

Although the Fylde Coast has seen several serious plane crashes in its time, few have been within the Blackpool boundaries. This RAF plane came down at Squires Gate in fog during the Second World War.

The world's first permanent electric street tramway opened in Blackpool on September 29, 1885. The line ran from Cocker Street to South Shore.

Overhead trolley trams were introduced in 1899.

The route today runs only along the seafront, with a small diversion inland at Manchester Square to the tramsheds, but it was not always so. Tramlines ran throughout the town in the late 19th century, along Church Street and Whitegate Drive, to Layton and to Marton. While other routes took them along Lytham Road and Waterloo Road to South Shore.

This picture shows the Norbreck Tram Stop early this century.

This was the Layton terminus, in Westcliffe Drive.

This group of men were all about to board the tram for the trial run of the Blackpool to Marton route in 1901.

Tram conductresses pictured during the 1914-18 war. Their wage was 25s for a 52-hour week.

When the trams ran past the South Shore sandhills, workmen were constantly having to clear the track beside the sand dunes. This picture dates from 1928.

The town's transport department publicised Blackpool's War Weapons Week in March 1941 by decorating this tram in patriotic style.

Tram buffs celebrated 75 years of trams in 1960.

*Tram posters such as this one
are now collectors' items.*

*Civic leaders gathered to say
goodbye to this tram, sold to
Massachusetts in March
1955.*

This tram trundled along Dickson Road, North Shore, in the '20s.

The Blackpool Belle, built in 1959, took the form of a Mississippi paddle steamer during the annual Illuminations. Her last official tour was in 1979 and this picture was the last before she was carried away to retirement in the Glenwood Trolley Park, Oregon, USA.

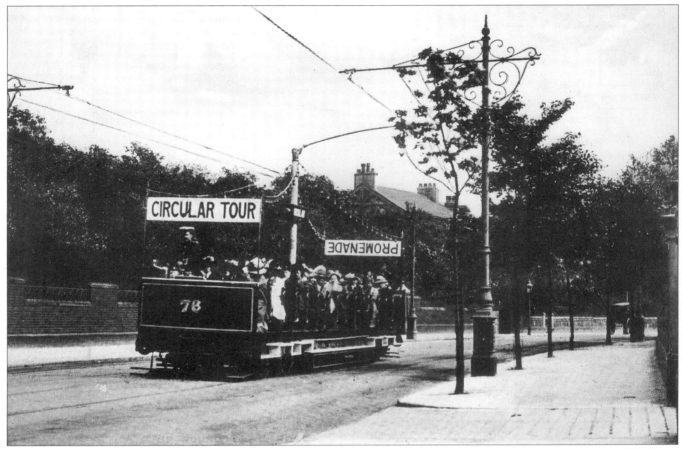

The so-called toastrack trams were Blackpool's answer to the charabanc when they were first introduced in 1911. The trams started the first circular tour of the town.

The rival. This 'run-a-bout' charabanc took passengers from the seafront along Hornby Road to the new park in the '20s. More than 30 people could be accommodated in these early charas.

After the First World War, the motor coach trade began to expand in earnest. The Smith family, who had started out using horse-drawn transport, were among the first to move into the motor vehicle trade. This was their Daimler charabanc loading up at the Hornby Road garage, ready to set off for Fleetwood.

The cars might be vintage – but the photograph is not. Take a look at the fashions. This was the final stretch of the annual Manchester-Blackpool vintage car rally, which still takes place today, in 1963.

Blackpool at War

Black Friday – September 1, 1939. This was how the Blackpool Evening Gazette broke the news that Germany had invaded Poland. Within 48 hours, Prime Minister Chamberlain had told the British people they were once more at war.

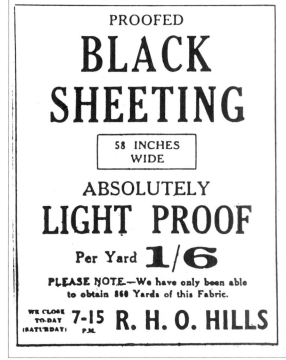

PROOFED

BLACK SHEETING

58 INCHES WIDE

ABSOLUTELY

LIGHT PROOF

Per Yard **1/6**

PLEASE NOTE.—We have only been able to obtain 860 Yards of this Fabric.

WE CLOSE TO-DAY (SATURDAY) **7-15** P.M. **R. H. O. HILLS**

Shops had to close early in winter because of the black-out and light-proof sheeting could be bought from the local stores, such as RHO Hills in Bank Hey Street.

BLACKPOOL CO-OPERATIVE SOCIETY LTD.

•

WAR EMERGENCY

RESTRICTION OF LIGHTING

To meet this the Shops of the Society will CLOSE EACH DAY as follows:

MONDAY - 6-0 o'clock p.m.
TUESDAY - 6-0 o'clock p.m.
WEDNESDAY 1-0 o'clock p.m.
(FOR WEEKLY HALF DAY HOLIDAY)
THURSDAY 6-0 o'clock p.m.
FRIDAY - 7-0 o'clock p.m.
SATURDAY 7-0 o'clock p.m.

We ask that our members will do all they can to assist us by shopping as early in the day as possible.

Sandbags, used nowadays to protect property from flood, were stored in readiness to await the German bomb attacks.

Evacuees were sent to Blackpool in their thousands. Being in the North West, it was considered less likely to face attack from the Germans than were towns in the south and east of England. It also had a ready-made supply of accommodation. More than 90,000 official evacuees were accommodated in more than 15,000 homes on the Fylde and more than 37,500 of these arrived during the first three days.
Some of the children had never been away from home before and only those under five were allowed to be accompanied by their mothers. For many, it was the first time they had seen the sea – and their first introduction to Blackpool.

This photograph, taken by former Gazette photographer Franklin N.Bain, was described by the Ministry of Information as one of the finest home-front pictures of the war, and went on to be reprinted all over the world. It shows three small sisters, evacuated from London in the flying bomb raids of 1944, sleeping peacefully in a Blackpool Methodist schoolroom.

The Women's Land Army was created to fill the jobs left vacant when the men went off to fight.

Water tanks were built all over Blackpool – including at North Pier.

Day nurseries became commonplace, as more children needed caring for.

The evacuees were allowed back home when the bombs failed to materialise, but returned in 1940 at the end of the blitz and again in 1944 when flying bombs were dropped on the south of England.

Hundreds of soldiers were billeted to Blackpool, which was Britain's biggest recruiting centre for the RAF, and entertainment was once again much in demand.

Civil servants, too, were relocated to Blackpool, while more than 20,000 American airmen took over the Warton airfield and worked on the assembly of fighters and bombers. Others, based at Burtonwood near Warrington, came to see the sea – and the girls.

At its peak, Blackpool had more than 60,000 servicemen in town, crammed into the guesthouses and small hotels.

George Formby, the Fylde's most famous entertainer, travelled the world entertaining the troops while the Tower Ballroom was the hub of local entertainment – and the venue for many a local lass to link arms with an attractive GI.

Rationing was introduced in January 1940 – and did not end until July 1954, nine years after the war ended.

Families began growing their own food wherever possible – but water, clothing and petrol were other items soon to face restrictions.

Queues at the Blackpool Food Office in October 1939.

Scrap metal, paper, rags and rubber products were collected and recycled to make airmen's dinghies, cartridge cases, oxygen masks, rubber petrol tanks and a host of other worthy items for war service. These girls organised their own collection in South Shore, in July 1940.

The blackout put an end to Blackpool Illuminations during the war years and, to help people find their way, white lines were painted on trees, kerbs and lamp-posts. This picture was taken in Harrowside, South Shore, in September 1939.

Blackpool suffered surprisingly few bomb attacks, considering the Tower and three piers were easy landmarks to spot, even in the blackout.

In total, there were nine attacks, in the autumn of 1940 and spring of 1941.

The first bombs fell on August 29, 1940, when two high explosive bombs fell on North Shore golf course.

The worst attack came in September that year, when nine bombs were dropped on North Station, killing eight people and injuring 14 others – the sum total of Blackpool's air-raid casualties.

One unexploded bomb fell on the railway line while another damaged part of the railway wall. The remainder razed nearby Seed Street.

This was the scene in Lindale Gardens and Farringdon Avenue, South Shore, after a bomb fell on October 19, 1940.

With men aged 18-41 enlisted for military service, women were called upon for a variety of previously-unknown tasks. They found themselves helping with civil defence, womens' auxiliary services, nursing, munitions, domestic work and in the transport services. Although they were not conscripted at first, by December 1941, the Government had decreed that all unmarried women aged 20-30 must either join the auxiliary services or work in industry.
These valiant ladies, pictured in May 1941, formed part of civil defence canteen staff.

Barricades were built on the Promenade at Blackpool during the War, while signs pointed the way to the nearest air raid shelters, should they be needed in the event of attack.

Women found themselves working in a variety of roles. These were pictured on the railways, carting heavy sacks of flour and other provisions in warehouses along the sidings.

There was a civic welcome in July 1942 for the commander of Blackpool's adopted ship HMS Penelope. Captain A.D.Nicholl CBE, DSO, RN, remained at his post on the bridge despite being wounded during the Malta raids. He is pictured inspecting the town's Sea Cadet Corps, who formed the guard of honour outside the Town Hall.

Above: This was the scene outside Blackpool Town Hall during Dig for Victory Week in March 1943. Illuminations engineer Mr F.W.Field designed the mural

Centre: A month later – Wings for Victory Week.

Bottom: Some members of the Home Guard did indeed bear similarities to the characters in the '70s TV sitcom Dad's Army! This picture, which appeared in the Gazette of December 21, 1940, shows volunteer stretcher bearers at work. On the left are special police and on the right, auxiliary firemen.

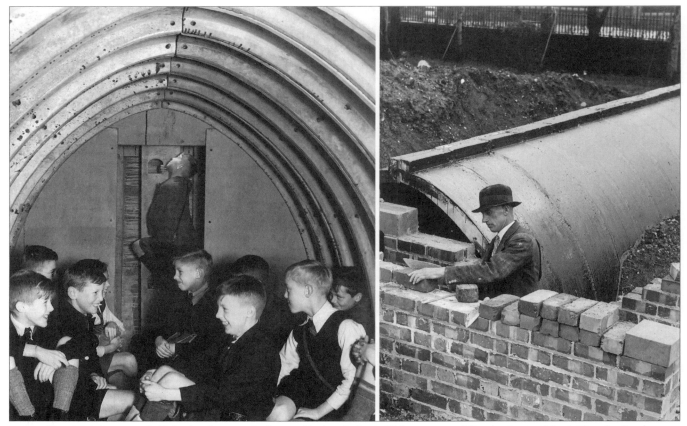

Air raid shelters were built in the playgrounds of many Blackpool schools. This one was at Waterloo Junior School, Waterloo Road.

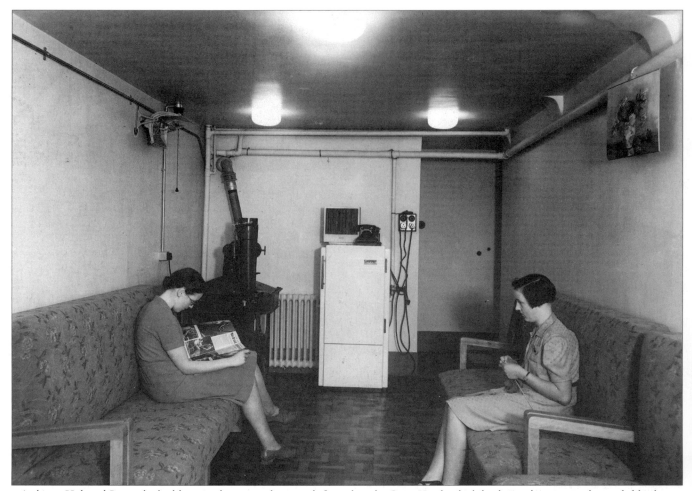

Architect Halstead Best, who had been in the news only a year before when the Gynn Hotel, which he designed, was opened, revealed his latest scheme – an air raid shelter in the garden of his Park Drive home.

All men between 20 and 23 had to report to the employment exchange to register for military service. This picture, taken in 1939, shows some members of the Blackpool battery of the royal artillery, ready to leave for duty.

Trenches were busily dug on the cliffs by members of the ARP.

A battery of 116 ARP trailer pumps were delivered to Blackpool's fire brigade headquarters in August 1938.

One of the most efficient ARP shelters was built in the warehouse of Blackpool Co-operative Society in Charnley Road.

The Blackpool Girls' Anchor League, the sister movement of the Sea Cadets, was the only one in the country when this parade took place on October 2, 1943.

Boys aged between 16 and 18, able to ride cycles and motorcycles, were accepted as messengers for the Auxiliary Fire Service.

The forces relied heavily on their canteens. This one, at the Queen Street Servicewomen's Club, was run by the Catholic Women's League.

These canteen vans were set to leave Blackpool in November 1940 to help sustain the troops.

The Yanks are coming …American GIs parade along Talbot Road in 1945.

VE Day – May 8, 1945. Talbot Square was awash with faces rejoicing at the news war with Germany was over.

*Victory! Blackpool puts
out its flags of victory on
VJ Day, in August
1945.*

*This group gathered in Dale
Street, off Chapel Street to
celebrate the news that Japan
was ready to surrender.*

Former Prime Minister Winston Churchill, who led Britain throughout the conflict, visited Blackpool at the end of the war, in September 1946, when he was granted the Freedom of the Borough. Seated beside him in the car is the then-Mayor of Blackpool, Cllr Frank Nickson MBE.

Famous Faces

There can be few celebrities able to claim they have never been to Blackpool. Not that they are likely to want to. For Blackpool has long been recognised as the springboard to stardom for many a budding entertainer. Theatres sprang up in abundance at the end of the last century, as the number of trippers to Blackpool increased. No holiday was complete without taking in a traditional summer show — something which still holds true today.

Top left: Laurel and Hardy came to Blackpool three times during their fun-filled career. Their first visit to England – and Blackpool – was in 1932, when more than 10,000 people packed the streets to see them, making what should have been a two-minute journey from their rooms at the Metropole Hotel to the Winter Gardens a marathon 20-minute ride. This picture was taken as they left town by train. They were not to return again until 1947.

REGINALD DIXON
Top right: This was the public face of Mr Blackpool, as known and loved by millions. He was presented with this replica of the Tower by Music for Pleasure records, when sales of his last long-playing record topped 50,000, in February 1969. Middle: This was the more private face, some 32 years earlier, when he and wife Vera were captured on camera with daughter Jacqueline, then aged two. Bottom: This picture, taken at Tarn Hows, the popular Lakeland beauty spot, shows Reg in a quiet moment with his daughters, at the end of the Second World War.

There were three things that visitors to Blackpool had to do in the '30s and '40s …

eat fish and chips out of newspaper on the Golden Mile, go to the top of the Tower and listen to Reginald Dixon in the Tower Ballroom.

Sunday concerts in the summer attracted packed houses, while the winter months saw him busy recording broadcasts for the masses nationwide.

Sheffield-born Reg began visiting Blackpool as a boy, little knowing that one day it would be both his home and source of his world-famous reputation!

He was appointed Tower organist in 1930 and tickled the Tower ivories for more than 40 years, taking the sound of the famous WurliTzer around the world.

He played regularly with the Tower Band under the direction of Bertini and went on to be featured with other big band names such as Geraldo, Billy Ternent, Joe Loss and Ted Heath.

He even proposed to his wife Vera on the balcony of the Ballroom, long before he ever played there as resident organist.

Reg was 65 in October 1969 and decided to call it a day at the keyboards.

His only concert after the '69 season was that designed specifically for his farewell.

The Tower Ballroom was packed to capacity on Easter Sunday 1970 for the concert, which was broadcast to the nation the following day. It was undoubtedly the end of an era.

He died in 1985, at the age of 80.

JOSEF LOCKE pictured here with comedian Frank Randle, signing a £1,000-a week contract with agent Jack Taylor in August 1950.

The Irish-born tenor made Blackpool his second home for a time, after marrying local lass Doreen McMartin in 1947. The marriage was short-lived and tragic, with the couple losing two of their infant daughters. This memorial to them still stands in Layton cemetery. Locke later returned to live in his native Eire and the marriage was dissolved in the 1950s, after it turned out to have been bigamous.

FRANK RANDLE, born poor and illegitimate in 1901, made and lost several fortunes during his career. At his peak, he was reputed to be the highest-paid performer in the country. He was forever in court and once admitted that some of his best performances were for Blackpool magistrates. He once hired an aeroplane and bombarded the town with toilet rolls, as revenge for being accused of on-stage obscenity. He is pictured here at his Blackpool home in 1952, with his pets Patsy and Fifi.

CLIFF RICHARD was a regular at Blackpool in the '60s and early '70s. He is pictured here opening a YMCA autumn fair in 1961. Cliff played the Opera House in 1961 and was the first person to top the bill at the newly-opened ABC, on the site of the old Hippodrome, in 1963.

SHIRLEY BASSEY, the songstress from Tiger Bay, was in town in July 1961. She returned in 1994 to switch on the illuminations.

Above: COUNT BASIE played the Palace Theatre in 1957.

Above: BETTE DAVIS The Hollywood legend came to Blackpool to escape the crowds, during her first visit to England in September 1936.
She booked into the County Hotel under her real name of Mrs H.O.Nelson, of California but was captured on camera by the Gazette as she strolled along the seafront.

Left: CHARLIE CHESTER, pictured on the right, is seen here with broadcaster Len Marten during the first of a series of BBC recordings at the Jubilee Theatre, Blackpool, of the 'Stand Easy' Show. Chester was awarded the MBE in 1990.

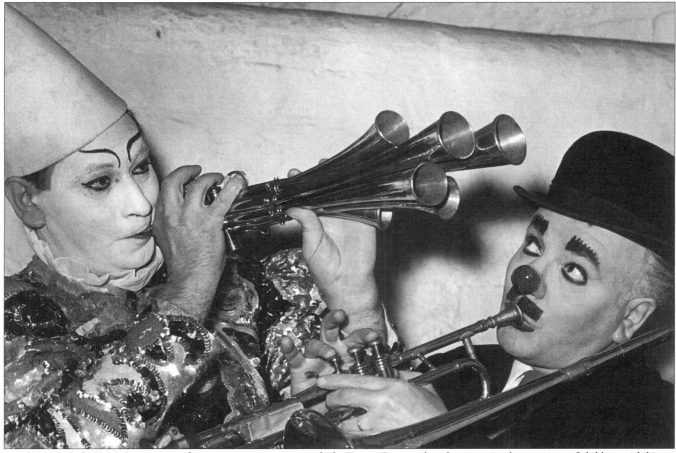

CHARLIE CAIROLI's name – and nose – was synonymous with the Tower Circus, where he entertained generations of children with his clowning around. He died in 1980, but son Charlie jnr. still carries on the family traditions. This photograph was taken at the Tower in 1958.

'OUR' GRACIE FIELDS and her husband Boris Alperovici visited Blackpool on many occasions. An early snap from 1927 captures her on one of the resort's famous donkeys. Later on, she braved the lion's den at the Tower Zoo, in search of Albert, that infamous son of Mr and Mrs Ramsbottom.

STANLEY HOLLOWAY, who immortalised Albert and the Lion, is pictured here with Leslie Henson, having 'urned' himself a cuppa at the YMCA canteen in Blackpool's Hippodrome theatre, in 1941.

Lancashire-born THORA HIRD is still a popular TV favourite, having launched her career in Blackpool.
She appeared with comedians Max and Syd Harrison in Saturday Night at the Crown, at the Grand Theatre in 1956, and again in 1962 in The Best Laid Schemes. In 1965, she again appeared at the Grand, this time with FREDDIE FRINTON in My Perfect Husband.

JIMMY JEWEL and BEN WARRISS performed together as a comedy act for 33 years and headlined spectacular shows at the old Hippodrome and Opera House.

Forties favourite NAT JACKLEY appeared in many a summer show in Blackpool. This impromptu performance in 1947 caught the "rubber neck" attempting to plough a furrow on Blackpool beach!

Hello Playmates! Yes – it's got to be ARTHUR ASKEY, pictured on Blackpool sands in 1953.
He spent many summer seasons in Blackpool, where he first met up with Jewel and Warriss.

VIOLET CARSON, probably better known as Coronation Street's cantankerous Ena Sharples, lived for most of her life in Blackpool.
She is pictured here on an 1899 Star Vis-à-Vis at the Royal Lancashire Showground after the Manchester to Blackpool vintage car run of 1967.

Right: JOHN TILLER – the founder of the Tiller Girls, whose dancers were regular visitors to the town at the height of showtime.

Far right: Blackpool has been hosting conferences for decades. Delegates to the 1927 Labour conference included the diminutive Miss Ellen Wilkinson MP. It was the beginning of life in politics for women.

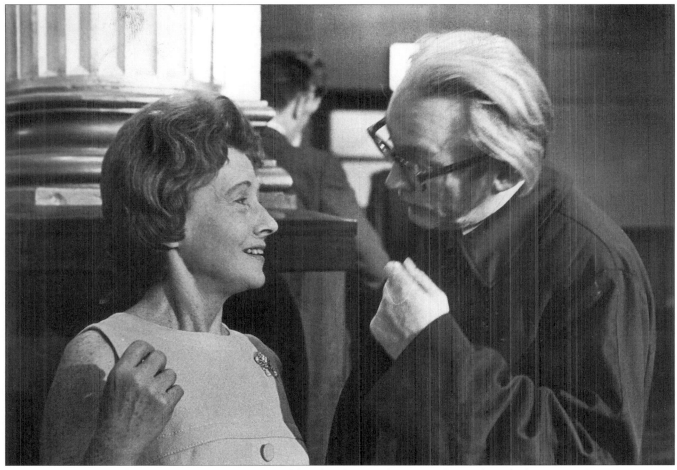

Her vociferous successors were to include the likes of Barbara Castle MP, seen here with Michael Foot in 1968.

There were none of today's security problems in the '70s, when top politicians were able to mingle freely with the masses. Since the Brighton bombing of 1984, delegates are more likely to find themselves with this kind of a welcome.

Prime Minister Harold Wilson and wife Mary are pictured outside the Winter Gardens in 1975.

Five years before, the bachelor PM Edward Heath was captured on camera as he danced with young conservative ball chairman Susan Hargreaves at the Locarno Ballroom, Central Drive.

Switch On Celebrities

The Duke of Kent is the only royal to have switched on the Lights – seen here in 1937, with the then town clerk, Trevor Jones.

Wilfrid Pickles in 1950.

Gilbert Harding in 1954.

The only four-legged switch-flicker was Red Rum in 1977.

George Formby, who immortalised the little stick of Blackpool rock, was an obvious choice for the 1953 switch-on.

Actress Jayne Mansfield added a touch of glamour to the proceedings in 1959.

Squadron leader Ginger Lacey (left), group captain Douglas Bader (right) and actor Patrick Wymark paid their own tribute to the Battle of Britain by switching on the Lights in 1969.

Sir Matt Busby in 1968.

The first Illuminations display was on Princess Parade in May, 1912. It was to mark the first Royal Visit to Blackpool, by Princess Louise, who officially opened the new section of the Promenade, subsequently known as Princess Parade. Due to popular demand, they were repeated the following year.

It was only really after the First World War, in 1925, that the business of Blackpool Illuminations really began to sparkle, thanks to this man, Fred Field.

It was another 10 years before the idea of having a switch-on ceremony, with celebrity guest, was introduced.

Dr Who? Actor Tom Baker blasts off in 1982.

Celebrities Year-by-Year

1934	Lord Derby
1935	Audrey Mosson (Railway Queen)
1936	Sir Josiah Stamp
1937	Alderman Ashton (later to be Duke of Kent)
1938	Cllr Mrs Quayle
1939-49	Cancelled due to the War
1949	Anna Neagle
1950	Wilfrid Pickles
1951	Stanley Matthews
1952	Valerie Hobson
1953	George Formby
1954	Gilbert Harding
1955	Jacob Malik (Russian Ambassador)
1956	Reginald Dixon
1957	John H.Whitney (American Ambassador)
1958	Matty Matthews
1959	Jayne Mansfield
1960	Janet Munro
1961	Violet Carson
1962	Shirley Ann Field
1963	Cliff Michelmore
1964	Gracie Fields
1965	David Tomlinson and cast of Mary Poppins
1966	Ken Dodd
1967	Dr Horace King
1968	Sir Matt Busby
1969	Canberra Bomber
1970	Tony Blackburn
1971	Cast of Dad's Army
1972	Danny la Rue
1973	Gordon Banks
1974	Wendy Craig
1975	Tom Baker (Dr Who)
1976	Miss UK Carol Ann Grant
1977	Red Rum
1978	Terry Wogan
1979	Kermit the Frog and the Muppets
1980	Cannon and Ball
1981	Earl and Countess Spencer
1982	Rear Admiral Sandy Woodward
1983	Cast of Coronation Street
1984	Johannes Rau and David Waddington MP
1985	Joanna Lumley
1986	Les Dawson
1987	Frank Bough, Ann Gregg & Kathy Tayler (Holidays)
1988	Andrew Lloyd-Webber and Sarah Brightman
1989	Frank Bruno
1990	Julie Goodyear & Roy Barraclough (Bet & Alec)
1991	Judith Chalmers & Derek Jameson
1992	Lisa Stansfield
1993	Status Quo
1994	Shirley Bassey

From just a few bulbs and strings of lights across the seafront, Blackpool Illuminations have grown into an annual spectacle of colour, which attracts visitors from all over the world – truly, the greatest free show on earth.

This tram was illuminated especially to honour Her Majesty the Queen in Coronation Year, 1953.

Last, but not least, there are Blackpool's sporting heroes.
The first seaside club to make it to the First Division, Blackpool could
proudly boast of players like Stanley Matthews, Stan Mortensen and
Jimmy Armfield in its halcyon days.

Sporting Heroes

Who would have thought
this timid-looking 11-year
old would go on to be
named footballer of the year
in both 1948 and 1963?
Stanley Matthews began his
brilliant career with Stoke
City, but transferred to
Blackpool for the princely
sum of £11,000 in 1947.

He played in the historic FA Cup Final against Bolton at Wembley in 1953 and is pictured on the Town Hall steps with team captain Harry Johnston in their moment of glory. Johnston, pictured inset with Matthews, following the game, was the youngest Blackpool player to appear in the First Division, being signed on his 17th birthday. He went on to become Blackpool's captain for nine successive post-war seasons and played in three Wembley Cup Finals before becoming manager of Reading.

This was the pass which helped Blackpool score the winning goal.

A formidable trio met up again in 1960 when they took part in the Tom Finney Testimonial. Pictured from left are Stanley Matthews, Tom Finney, Jimmy Armfield and Stan Mortensen.

Golden goalscorer Jimmy Hampson worked in the coal pits before signing for Blackpool from Nelson in 1927. A brilliant player, he made 360 appearances for Blackpool and scored 247 league goals – 45 of which were in one season (1929-30) alone.

Hampson died tragically, aged only 32, when a yacht on which he was aboard collided with a trawler off Fleetwood on January 14th, 1938.

Jimmy Armfield, who, with 43, is the most-capped Blackpool player, captained Blackpool for 13 years up to 1971. He is pictured here with Morty at the FA Centenary Dinner at the Grosvenor Hotel, London.

Blackpool Football Club held an annual dinner with directors of the old Blackpool Tower Company. Players and officials, left to right, on the back row are: Fred Jones (club secretary), Leslie Lea, Mandy Hill, Neil Turner, Gordon West, Bruce Crawford, Ray Parry, Ian Cuthbert, David Durie, Bill Perry, Des Horne, Ray Charnley, Jimmy Armfield, Eric Hayward, coach, and Roy Gratrix.
The various directors on the second row from the front are, left to right: Ron Suart (Blackpool manager), Charles Gaulter (Tower and BFC), Eric Cunliffe (BFC), Frank Evans (BFC), F.Herbert Grime (BFC), Rhodes Marshall (BFC) — , Albert Hindley (BFC chairman), Douglas Bickerstaffe (Tower chairman), Dick Seed (BFC), Albert Stuart (BFC), Dr Alec Bruce (club doctor), Johnny Lynas (club physio and director), Dr James Sime (club doctor), Dr Ken Shepherd (club dentist and director) and Sir Harold Grime, editor-in-chief of the Evening Gazette.

Although Brian London kept the surname made famous by his boxing father Jack, it was a Blackpool-born lad, not a Londoner, who went on to become the British and Empire Champion. His sparring career took him all over the world. He is pictured here in one of his later clashes with Muhammed Ali, earlier known as Cassius Clay, at the Odeon, Leicester Square, in 1966.

Subscribers

Presentation copy:

The Mayor of Blackpool

Bessie Aikman
Brenda Aitken
Charles Aldersley
Mark J Andrew
Paul R Andrew
David & Michelle Angel
Margaret Ansell
Averil Appleby
Jimmy Armfield
Michael S Arnold
P R Ashmore
Arthur Ashton
G E Atkinson
Kirk Atkinson
Millie Atkinson
Mrs M Bacon
Mr Alan G Bagot
J & Q Bamber
Barry Band
Andrew Barker
Cedric Barker
John Barker
Cis Baron
Revd D J Barrett
John Barton-Rossall
J R H Battersby
      (Mayor of Blackpool 1985-86)
Mr William Bee
Rita Beighton
Stephen Beilby JP, DL
Terence Beresford
Ronald Berkley
Kenneth R Berry
Steve Betts
Joe Bird
S Birtwistle
Paul W Boddis
Michael Philip Bolton
Peter Booth
Mrs Sheila Maureen Boyes
John Frank Bradley
Mrs M Bradbury
Muriel Bradshaw
Mrs N Breeze
Henry Brindle
Dr Vernon Broadhurst
Vernon Broadhurst
James C L Bromley
Valerie Brook
Mr H Brown
Olive Yvonne Brown
Sylvia & Cliff Brown
Joyce M Bruce
R Buckley
Frank Burgess
Michael Burnett
T H Burns
L Butterworth
Paul Buttery
Mrs N Campion
Gina M V Cardwell

A E Carter
Mrs Margaret Chapman
Mrs Sheila Chappell
Gordon A Clark
K E R Clarke
Albert Clayton
Mr Wm G Clee
Mrs May Clowes
Freda M Cockcroft
Tommy M Coe
Fred Coleman
Gill & Derek Connell
David Cook
A Cooke
R Cooke
Mr H Cooper
John Terence Cooper
Tom Courtenay
Mr & Mrs H Cousins
Mr James Cox
Crackousrockanroll
Thomas Crankshaw
Cricketland Kindergarden
G K Crook
Alan Cross
Mr Carl Cross
David F Cross
Mavis Cross
Raymond Cross
E Dabbs
W R Dagger
Bill Dainty
George Dale
Malcolm & Jill Dando
Robert Darch
Mr G Davidson
Carol Davies
H M Davies
Jead Davies
C Davison
Mrs G Dawes
P Day
Patricia Deakin
David Dean
John Deans
Mrs E D Dewhurst
Frances Ditzel
Stephanie Donaldson
Isobel Donnelly
David A Dougill
Ann Douglas
Mr & Mrs E A Doyle
Charles G Drayton
Pamela Drew
Barry Durham
P B Eaves
Richard Eaves
Mary M Edwards
W E Ellis
K J Evans
Mrs Margaret Fairclough

Tony Fairclough
Mr Fred Farley
Margaret Farnen
Catherine Farrar
Michael S Farrar
Mr Z N J Faulkher-Cavney
Russell Fellows
Mrs B Fenton
Miss M Fenton
Miss D T Field
J R Fielding
B & E Firth
R Fishwick
Robin Fletcher
Mr & Mrs G Fortt
Victor Foster
Mr G A & Mrs J Fowler
Iris W French
E H Funk
Mr Christopher Gahan
Mr Cyril Gallimore
Miss N T Gazey
Steve & Margaret Gerrard
Mrs M L Gill
Anthea Giller
Conor, Sean & Peter Gilligan
Dick Gillingham
Tommy Givanovich
Jacqueline & Kenneth Gooch
R Goodall
M Grabiec
Russell Grant
L A Green
Walter J Green
J M Greener
Joan Greenhalgh
N O Gregg
Mrs Yvonne Gregitis
Peter Griffin
Miss E Gunby
J R Hague
John Victor Halstead
Mr & Mrs David Hammond
Margaret E Hampson
John Leonard Hancock
Mr Peter S Hardman
Miss Audrey Hargreaves
Mr Michael Harrington
Bernice Harrison
Mr Denis Harrison
Kenneth 'Harry' Harrison
Margaret Harrison
Mr Stanley Eric Harrison
Stephen John Harvey
Mrs D Harwood
Mr Peter K Hay
Mr C J Hayward
James David Healey
Lynda Heaton
The Herons Nest
Susan J Higginson

Mrs Elsie Hill
Joan & Don Hill
Mr & Mrs J O Hilton
Kenneth Hitchen
F S Hogg
Mark Holdcroft
T S Holden
Guy Holloway
Mr Kenneth F Holmes
Barbara D Holt
Margaret Holyoake
Mr & Mrs Alistair Hope
Mr & Mrs Geoffrey Hope
Mr & Mrs Robert Hope
Mr & Mrs Steven Hope
Herbert Horabin
Brian Hornby
Edward Hornby
Arthur Horrocks
Olga Horsfall
Arthur W Houghton
S M & J A Houghton
W Roy Houghton
Kathleen Howard
R Howard
R Howard
Derek Hoyle
D C Huckvale
E Hudson
Norman Colgrave Huttley
Kenneth Jackson
Mrs M Jackson
Peter A Jackson
R Jackson
R Jackson
Stanley Jenkinson
Barbara Johnson
Mrs Ada Jones
Mr & Mrs H Jones (Taree, Australia)
Mr & Mrs L K Jones (Blackpool)
Peter M V Jones
Thomas Jones
Mr B Keeling
L G Kelshaw
Mr Peter Kenniford
George King
Peter Knowles
Mr & Mrs K Knudsen
Mrs I Lahiff
Anne & Jack Lamb
P Lamont
Lancashire Family History & Heraldry
     Society (Fylde Branch)
Peter D Lancaster
Mr D S Lane
Mrs E Latham
Vera Lee
Alan John Lees
K H Lewis
Ted Lightbown
Mr V Linden
Mrs E Lister
Mrs Olive Littler
Raymond Lloyd
Longfellow Office Supplies
Mr N Longton
Robert David Lucas
Mr V S Lund
Mr F Lyons
Eric McBrine
Michael M McCarthy
Jane M McDonnell

Kathleen McKearnen
Frank McKnight
J A McNicholl
John Maher
A P Maitland
D E Manson
M Mason
Mrs Dorothy Mercer
Howard & Catherine Merrill
Frank Metcalfe
Hannah Millard
Mr S W Milne
Harold Monks
Jean Moore
John Moore
William Moore
Moor Park Junior School
Barry Morris
Kenneth G Morris
Susan Dorothy Moses
Ian M Moss
Mrs Lillian Moss
Colin Moxey
John Muncaster
H Myers
Eileen, Tom & Alan Mylecraine
Mr & Mrs A Naylor
Sue Naylor
Dorothy M Notton
Derek S Ormond
Miss S A Osgood
Edith M Owen
John Padden
Mr Damien Page
Bryan J Palmer
Brenda Parker JP
John Barrie Parker
Ada Parkinson
Kenneth Parkinson
Ernest Pashley
Doris Peers
Mary Pendleton
K Pennington
Marion Percival
James Perkins
Carol & Vin Peterson
David Philpott
William C Platt
G Raby
Edward Ratcliffe
Mrs J E Reid
Mr & Mrs B P Reynolds
Jean Richardson
Margaret Rimmer
Mrs D M Roberts
Beverley Robinson
C Robinson
Anne Roome
Mrs D Roscow
Mr & Mrs K & D M Rose
Graham Ross
Mrs M Ross
Mr & Mrs A H Rossall
C R Sagers
W Savage
Carole Scarlett
Stan & Mollie Schofield
Mrs V Schofield
Mrs C M Scott
Margaret Seaman
Kay & Roy Sharp (New Zealand)
John Shaw

Tony Shaw
Kenneth Shenton
Geoff Sherwood
Paul Shipton
Mary Shone
Mrs Doreen Singleton
Edwina Singleton
Mark Steven Singleton
Audrey Slater
Mrs Andrea Smith
Bill Smith (Haulage)
Margaret Snowden
Joan Spence
James Stanhope
M J & I G Stevens
Mr J Stirk
Mrs Barbara Stone
Chiquita Sunley
Peter Swift
Mr Robert Swift (Australia)
Mrs H Swinton
C G Tarr
Bert Taylor
Brian Taylor
Claire Jayne Taylor
Edward Thompson
Mrs J Tolliday
Margaret Tomlinson
Mr Arthur E Turner
Michael J Turner
Richard M Turner
David Upton
Dr K S Vasudev
Mr & Mrs Wadsworth
Gerald Walkden
K F Walker
Ruth Walker
Ian Walsh
Mr Ralph Walsh
Mr & Mrs T E Walsh
Clifford Warburton
Graham Ward
Eunice Ward
Ian & Erica Ward
Rita & Malcolm Ward
Leslie Craig Warren
Eileen Wasley
C Watson-Harrison
H Graham Weaver
Mr K Weigh
Mrs Kathleen Whiston
Irene T Wilkinson
Marie Williams
Mrs I Williams
Mrs Joan M Williams
Norman Wilson
Hilda M Windsor
Mrs Margaret Wiseman
Walter Wolstenholme
Anthony Wood
Joyce Wood
Paul Wood
Ronald Arnold Wood
John M Woollard
Barbara Wright
J P Wright
Susan Yates (née Barlow)
Elené Yates
Edmund Yorke
Alan & Barbara Young